I did not intend to read this book, but t
What a relief: a young-adult faith mem
Andrea Palpant Dilley is refreshingly,
being angsty or impossibly pious. She has
tions, bottom-line questions, and at the end of the day she leaves room
for a faith where everything doesn't have to be tied together with a neat
Jesus-y bow. Instead, Dilley raises the possibility—the *hope*—that honest
Christian faith has loose ends, and that God is fine with that. By the end
of the book, I wanted more of both God and Andrea Dilley.

> — KENDA CREASY DEAN, professor of youth, church, and culture,
> Princeton Theological Seminary; author of *Almost Christian:*
> *What the Faith of Our Teenagers Is Telling the American Church*

Truth. Reality. Meaning. Where do we find these elusive treasures in a
skewed, surreal, and often seemingly meaningless world of unspeakable
suffering? In this story of her young life, Andrea Palpant Dilley, missionary child and modern woman, struggles with these great questions in
such an honest, literate, and engaging way that the reader is swept into
her story as a fellow searcher for truth. Like all of us, she still struggles to
find all the answers. But she has learned where "tires are fixed" on the
journey. I believe that in this book we are witnessing the birth of a major
contemporary writer.

> — FREDERICK DALE BRUNER, Wasson Professor of Theology Emeritus,
> Whitworth University; author of *The Gospel of Matthew* and *The Gospel of John*

After summiting Mount Rainier, John Muir wrote to his wife, "I did not
mean to climb it, but got excited and soon was on top."That's how I felt
when I finished reading *Faith and Other Flat Tires* during a very busy week.
Seldom have I been so touched by the truth and ache of a spiritual memoir. Andrea Palpant Dilley's writing is fresh and clean and direct. You will
examine your own soul through hers.

> — PAUL J. WILLIS, author of *Bright Shoots of Everlastingness:*
> *Essays on Faith and the American Wild*

Andrea Dilley's literary stroll down her own particular path of faith
reminds us that while that way is narrow, it is also, at times, rather curvy
and fraught with obstacles. Her winsome recollections are a balm for
anyone walking a similar journey.

> — TRACY BALZER, author of *Thin Places: An Evangelical*
> *Journey into Celtic Christianity* and *A Listening Life*

Andrea compellingly writes a contemporary conversion narrative mixed with a cultural travelogue, as a representative of a generation that grew up in and struggled with one corner of the Christian landscape. It is written with a storyteller's ear and an English major's eye. For those who workaround the church, this is a must-read, to see the generation we long to reach.

— JIM SINGLETON, Senior Pastor, First Presbyterian Church,
Colorado Springs

With honesty and candor, Andrea Palpant shares her sense of displacement, as a "third-culture kid" finding her way in America and as a once-confident Christian beset with doubt and confusion in a postmodern world. I suspect many readers will find themselves in the questions that drive her away from faith. I also pray that, in her story, they will see a pathway back. At this time in our culture, and in the church, we are in need of people like Andrea, who do not shy away from their questions and doubts, who do not fear baring their souls, and who show us a way through to the other side of faith.

— STEVE SHERWOOD, Assistant Professor of Christian Ministry
George Fox University; and Young Life Regional Trainer

Andrea Palpant Dilley's bracingly honest memoir serves as an antidote both to the negative view of missionary families popularized by such books as *The Poisonwood Bible*, and to simplified stories of Christian conversion. Her unconventional story of reconversion, mapped against key events of *Pilgrim's Progress*, argues both for the unique trajectory of each individual experience and for shared themes in the long process of transformation. Her own rediscovery and embrace of her identity and community is shown, wisely, to be the starting point for what is "yet a long road in front of [her]." We hope that this fine and passionate young writer will take us along on her journey as it unfolds.

— MAXINE HANCOCK, Professor Emerita of Interdisciplinary Studies,
Regent College; author of *Gold from the Fire: Postcards from a Prairie Pilgrimage* and *The Key in the Window: Marginal Notes in Bunyan's Narratives*

FAITH AND OTHER FLAT TIRES

A MEMOIR

Searching for God
on the Rough Road of Doubt

Andrea Palpant Dilley

ZONDERVAN.com/
AUTHORTRACKER
follow your favorite authors

ZONDERVAN

Faith and Other Flat Tires
Copyright © 2012 by Andrea Palpant Dilley

This title is also available as a Zondervan ebook.
Visit www.zondervan.com/ebooks.

This title is also available in a Zondervan audio edition.
Visit www.zondervan.fm.

Requests for information should be addressed to:
Zondervan, *Grand Rapids, Michigan* 49530

Library of Congress Cataloging-in-Publication Data

Dilley, Andrea Palpant, 1978 –
    Faith and other flat tires : searching for God on the rough road of doubt /
    Andrea Palpant Dilley.
        p. cm.
    ISBN 978-0-310-32551-2 (softcover)
    1. Dilley, Andrea Palpant, 1978 – 2. Presbyterians — United States —
Biography.
    I. Title.
    BX9225.D53A3   2012
    285.092 — dc23   [B] 2011028930

Cover photography: Harri Tahvanainen / Getty Images®
Interior Photography: Andrea Palpant Dilley
Interior design: Katherine Lloyd

Printed in the United States of America

11 12 13 14 15 16 /DCI/ 20 19 18 17 16 15 14 13 12 11 10 9 8 7 6 5 4 3 2 1

Dedicated to Stephen,
my fellow pilgrim

By then I wasn't just asking questions;
I was being changed by them. I was being changed by
 my prayers,
which dwindled down nearer and nearer to silence . . .
I was a lost traveler wandering in the woods,
needing to be on my way somewhere but not knowing
 where.

—Wendell Berry, *Jayber Crow*

Contents

Foreword

Writing this foreword for Andrea is like showing the house you grew up in to good friends. To them it is simply a house, beautiful and comfortable, perhaps, but little more. But to you it is full of memory and meaning, a living repository of past relationships and events that shaped your life into what it is today.

Andrea is like that old house to me. She and I "have history." I have known her parents for more years than I dare count, and Andrea almost as long. My first clear recollection of her dates back to her senior year in high school, though I met her long before that. She enrolled in one of the classes I teach at Whitworth University. A year later, I asked her to serve as my part-time nanny to care for my children and to help with household responsibilities, which enabled me to stay on top of the challenges I faced as a widowed father of three. In this capacity, she also traveled with our family to Kenya during the summer of 2000. Later, at her wedding, I officiated and my children sang. Last year she read Scripture at my wedding. History indeed.

Still, I write this foreword not because we have history but because I want to introduce you to a promising young writer and her first book. It is a memoir, or what English departments these days call "creative nonfiction." The memoir genre is fraught with peril. For every memoir that works, many more fail. The medium has become predictable: author tells a sad tale of family problems and personal suffering, which turns said author into a victim or a victor, depending on the response. The competition for "most horrible background" seems fierce, thus proving the adage that it is easier to write about evil than it is to write about good.

Andrea's memoir is both different and as refreshing as her personality. She describes her background—family, mentors, church, relationships, experiences—with respect, affection, and realism, neither idealizing nor demonizing. As she makes plain, her background is not really the issue at all; as the word implies, it is like backdrop and props on a stage. Instead, she emphasizes what is in the foreground— her own struggle of faith, which she explores with honesty and wisdom. She is not a victim, but she is not always the victor, as you will see. She strikes a balance between telling a story that is both particular and universal, particular because it grew out of a set of circumstances unique to her, but also universal because it addresses what every human being on planet earth has to face sooner or later—the question of whether it is possible to believe in God while living in a very fallen, broken, confusing world.

She has done it well. She tells her story without becoming indulgent as a victim or preachy as the victor. She invites the reader in, saying, in effect, "This is my story. I present it to you as one person's struggle for faith." It is so carefully and seamlessly crafted that, though I began the book thinking about her story, I ended it thinking about my own. The shift happened so subtly and mysteriously I hardly knew it happened at all, except that suddenly I found myself reflecting on what faith means in ordinary life, how faith is forged, why it comes so hard for so many of us. As this book illustrates, good stories start out as windows and end up as mirrors. That Andrea has an uncommonly gracious heart, a good eye and an ear for language, a mind for detail, and patience to find the right word and turn the right phrase has helped to make this a fine book. Still, her skill, however impressive, is not really the point. Her ability to reflect on the past, to find meaning, and to see grace in people and events that seemed anything but gracious is what won me over. I suspect that it will win you over too.

It is my privilege, therefore, to introduce Andrea Palpant Dilley, to celebrate her rare talent and good heart, and to commend her book to you, which I suspect will be the first of many.

—Jerry Sittser
Spokane, Washington

Acknowledgments

The family in Kenya, 1980

First, I'd like to make a few quick notes to my reader. In telling my own story, I depict other people's stories too. As such, I have taken measures to respect privacy. For those individuals with whom I am still in contact, I have provided them with the opportunity to review and approve the material written here. After approving the story, some have opted to have their names changed, while others have chosen to keep their real names. For those with whom I am no longer in contact, names have been altered to protect their privacy. Personal descriptions, minor event details, and minor location details have been changed, as well.

Most of the dialogue in the book is derived from detailed journal entries, the rest I have recalled vividly from memory or have reconstructed with the assistance of those who took part in the dialogue. I have done the best I can to remember events and render them with accuracy. I have also done extensive fact-checking.

Although the book covers a range of experiences and relationships, it does not provide a comprehensive exposition of my theological views but instead focuses on key characters and events that best describe the arc of my spiritual story from childhood into my midtwenties. I frame my story by using John Bunyan's *The Pilgrim's Progress* as a parallel pilgrimage. The order of locations in Bunyan's work, however, has been rearranged to fit my own narrative.

Second, I am indebted to a great number of people for their help in getting this book off the ground:

For their time invested in reviewing the manuscript in its early, awkward stage, I would like to thank Brenna Robinson, Joy Crosby, Joy Lockard, Stephanie Lenox, Linda Hunt, Pamela Corpron Parker, Jerry Sittser, Andrew David, and Matt Newcomb. Their insightful feedback helped shape this story. For their assistance in fact-checking details in the manuscript, I would like to thank Forrest Baird, John Yoder, Scott Edminster, Joel Crosby, Jed Crosby, Kathy Crosby, Joy Crosby, Kip Winans, Jeremiah Webster, Damian Westfall, Betsy Kamuka, Cathy Ashene, Barb Comito, Cathy Roginski, Tom Tiffany, Mike Helland, Sam Palpant, Judy Palpant, Benjamin Palpant, and Nathan Palpant.

I would like to thank Hannah Faith Notess for including

in the *Jesus Girls* anthology an essay of mine that became the seed for this memoir. My thanks to Linda Hunt for pushing me to write the book in the first place, Pam Parker for suggesting that I use *The Pilgrim's Progress* as a narrative framing device, Paul Moede for encouraging me, and Tim Beals from Credo Communications for reviewing my contract. I would also like to give a special thanks to Jerry Sittser, for his faithful support of this project in all of its stages. I am indebted to him.

I am very grateful to my editors at Zondervan for their partnership in this project. I would like to thank Angela Scheff for taking a risk with a new author and accepting my book proposal, Sandy Vander Zicht for being an advocate for and champion of this book for the last two years, and Brian Phipps for finessing the manuscript and being a creative sounding board in the final stages of the process. I am also grateful to Stacy Mattingly for collaborating so closely on the manuscript, giving such painstaking attention to detail, and being a cheerleader for a tired, sleep-deprived mother/writer.

I am indebted to my mothers, Marti Smith and Judy Palpant, for their generous childcare support over the last two years, to my brothers for their love and support, and to my parents, for reading to me as a kid and instilling in me a love of books, language, and narrative. Finally, I am indebted to my husband, Stephen Dilley, who went the extra mile in supporting me. I am thankful to him for reading and critiquing the manuscript more times than I can count, doing mind-numbing research on my behalf, encouraging me, changing diapers and taking our kid to the park many, many times so I could write, and most important, being alongside me as a partner in this journey. This book is as much his as it is mine.

Introduction

STRIPPING OFF THE ICHTHUS

During my junior year in college, I took a butter knife from my mother's kitchen one afternoon and scraped the Christian fish decal off the back bumper of my Plymouth hatchback. The car was a tin can on wheels. The outside door handle on the driver's side came off in your hand sometimes, and the engine reeked of sulfur when you drove uphill. My older brother, Ben, had the car for a few years and drove his first girlfriend around in it. After he graduated from college, the car became mine.

On the back bumper, Ben had stuck one of those faux-chrome Ichthus decals that you can buy at Christian bookstores. I don't know what exactly prompted me to scrape it off, but I can still remember the series of steps I took in doing it. I pulled open the kitchen drawer, lifted a butter knife from the silverware tray, and then walked out into the street where the car was parked. Squatting near the tailpipe, I scratched off the fish decal and with relief watched it fall away in small flakes. I wanted the car as neutral space. I wanted an unmarked car as a symbol of an unmarked heart.

The reasons for my discontent were complicated. I wasn't raised by zealous, overbearing parents, and I didn't grow up in a hyper-conservative church. Roughly the first six years of my life were spent in East Africa, where my parents worked as Quaker medical missionaries. When I was seven, we moved to the Pacific Northwest and started attending a Presbyterian church that over the years gave me hymns and mission trips and potluck dinners. I grew up in a healthy Christian home and a healthy Christian community. And yet, beginning in adolescence, I started questioning everything I'd been raised to believe.

One of the stories of my Christian childhood was *The Pilgrim's Progress*, the allegory of faith written in 1678 by John Bunyan. In the story, Pilgrim (or "Christian") leaves behind his family and goes on a lifelong pilgrimage in search of heaven, the Celestial City. The characters—like Mr. Great Heart, Mr. Worldly Wiseman, and Obstinate—symbolize different qualities that either bolster or weaken a person's faith. The places—like Doubting Castle, the Slough of Despond, and the Hill of Difficulty—symbolize different episodes in a person's spiritual journey. My parents read *The Pilgrim's Progress* to my brothers and me when we were growing up. Sprawled out on my mother's lap, I would listen to her voice carry across countries of myth and imagination while Pilgrim went on his epic journey, slaying dragons and getting sucked into mud pits.

The story of *The Pilgrim's Progress* had a campy, otherworldly quality that I loved as a kid. But once I became a young adult, my own life more and more started to resemble Pilgrim's. I passed through episodes of doubt, faith, and despondency. Different people traveled with me along the various stretches of my journey. Never as straightforward as the characters in an allegory—conveniently named Charity and Help or Lord Hate-good and Beelzebub—the people in my life were less caricatured and more complex. Some of them turned me toward faith, some turned me away from faith, and some did both. Some traveled with me for discreet episodes and some for decades.

The most unsettling part of my pilgrimage took place during my early twenties, right after college. When people muse to me about how fondly they remember that era of their lives, I want to say, "What were you smoking back then, and what are you smoking now?" My twenties were marked mostly by disillusionment. After graduating, I worked four part-time jobs to pay the bills and lived alone for a time in an old apartment. I fell in love with complicated men—including someone twice my age who had a messy marriage history—and found myself perpetually brokenhearted. And I indulged the cliché rebellions of a Christian girl, experimenting with cigarettes, hanging out in bars, and drinking hard alcohol.

If I follow the standard testimonial conversion narrative for Christians, what I'm supposed to say next is that all of this "secularity" I experienced led me to question my faith. The script goes something like this:

Step 1: Grow up in a Christian church.

Step 2: Go off to college away from said church.

Step 3: Be exposed to the enticements of secular life.

Step 4: Try drugs and cigarettes and Pearl Jam.

Step 5: Leave the church because of so-called worldly enticements.

Step 6: Experience epiphany; realize vapidness of said secular things.

Step 7: Return to church with penitent heart.

Step 8: Reestablish faith, discover good living.

The pilgrimage is never that straightforward, at least not for most of us. The path I took both paralleled and deviated from this script and was motivated less by external influences and more by my own spiritual unrest.

During college, I thought of my struggle in terms of the literature I was reading. I discovered the southern Catholic writer Walker Percy and read his novel *The Moviegoer*, a less explicitly Christian, more contemporary version of *The Pilgrim's Progress*. In *The Moviegoer*, the main character, Binx Bolling, goes on what he calls "the search," roaming around the streets of New Orleans trying to find God and meaning in the modern malaise. He feels lost, listless, and alone.

Turn-of-the-century German poet Rainer Maria Rilke wrote too about "the search," but in different terms. During my senior year, one of my English professors read me a poem from Rilke's *Das Stundenbuch* (*A Book for the Hours of Prayer*). While I was sitting in the English lounge one afternoon, he came into the room carrying a book in that priestly way that professors do. He stood opposite me and began to read aloud:

Sometimes a man stands up during supper
and walks outdoors, and keeps on walking,
because of a church that stands somewhere in the East.

And his children say blessings on him as if he were dead.

And another man, who remains inside his own house,
stays there, inside the dishes and in the glasses,
so that his children have to go far out into the world
toward that same church, which he forgot.

I won't attempt to interpret the whole poem here. But in the first stanza, the man who walks out of the house seems to be going on a spiritual journey in search of God, just as Bunyan's Pilgrim does. I see my own story too as a pilgrimage. For me, though, the end point was always unclear. I didn't know whether I was leaving the church to find God or leaving my Christian childhood for a different kind of faith or something else entirely. Mostly I just felt confused. I progressed, regressed, retraced my steps, and got lost. If I were a Christian at all, then I was an Old Testament Christian prone to David's longing, Ruth's homelessness, and Solomon's love of beauty and dominion.

As a coming-of-age experience, my pilgrimage was motivated by three separate but concurrent desires for faith, love, and meaning. I was trying to find purpose in my work, a partner on my journey, and a worldview I could believe in. I felt compelled to search for God at the same time that I harbored serious doubts and questions: why does God seem distant? Why do people suffer? Why does the church seem dysfunctional? The questions started weighing down my heart like stones and eventually became too much for me to handle. At age twenty-three, I stepped over the threshold of the church and walked away. I had no idea if I would come back.

This book tells the story of what came of my search. It is written for people who, like me, find themselves driven by doubt and wandering the margins in search of a place to call home.

PART ONE

THE HOUSE OF THE INTERPRETER

A CHILDHOOD RETROSPECTIVE

The House of the Interpreter is a rest stop along the way, a type of spiritual museum providing guidance to Pilgrim and his companions on the road. It contains pictures and dioramas that portray aspects of the Christian faith and lessons on how to live the Christian life.

Chapter 1

MUNGU YU MWEMA

Me with Betsy Kamuka, upper left

One winter afternoon when I was twelve years old, my father picked up a hitchhiker. My two brothers were sitting with me in the back seat of our Plymouth Voyager van, which my grandfather had hauled off the junkyard and rebuilt. The cars we drove were all orphans that had been rolled or flooded or wrecked. The Voyager had a big dent in the sliding door from a downhill tumble.

The hitchhiker looked sixteen or seventeen, a tall Scandinavian wearing blue jeans with big holes in the knees. It was thirty-five degrees out. He ducked his head and climbed into the van with us, and then my dad drove on. The ensuing conversation, which I will never forget, went something like this:

"These are my kids, Andrea, Ben, and Nate. My name's Sam. What's your name?"

"Donovan," the hitchhiker said.

"Oh, that's a good name." My father paused. "Have you ever heard of Amy Carmichael?"

"Um, no ..."

"She was a Christian missionary to India who worked to save young girls from sex trade enslavement. The place where she worked was called Dohnavur, which is kind of close to your name, Donovan. So you have a good name, a name with Christian purpose."

"Oh."

In the hitchhiker's long pause that followed, I remember thinking, My father is out of his mind, preying on this young hitchhiker who wanted a ride and instead got a church sermon on Christian missionary history. I felt embarrassed in the same way I did when my dad prayed over our food in a restaurant and the waiter brought the ketchup while he was still praying.

Donovan rode with us for several miles until we reached the cut-off road to our house. After pulling the van onto the shoulder to let him out, my dad turned to my older brother, who was about the same size as the hitchhiker, and said, "Ben, why don't you give Donovan your jeans. It's cold out."

In the back seat of the van, Ben took off his pants and gave them to the hitchhiker while my little brother and I looked sideways at each other. Proverbial Christian wisdom says you give away the coat off your back, not the pants off your backside. In exchange for my brother's jeans, the hitchhiker handed over his own—the jeans with big holes in the knees—and my brother wrestled them on. Then Donovan got out. He was headed farther north toward Canada. I watched from the back seat as he diminished into the distance, a tall, lean figure standing on the side of a long winter road.

These years later, I remember the whole exchange as a small act of goodness. My father, the funny priest, blessed a hitchhiker not with holy water but with jeans. I can see this only in retrospect, though. Then, in my early teens, my mom and dad seemed painfully Christian and parental. After supper every night we had what was called "family time." We sometimes took walks in the woods or played card games, but more often than not, my dad directed us in an intellectual exercise of some kind. He would stride over to the living room bookshelves to find a book like *Les Misérables* by Victor Hugo, then read a passage aloud and try to engage us in dialogue. On occasion, he slid out one of the burgundy volumes of the Encyclopedia Britannica, which my mom had bought from a door-to-door salesman in the mid-1980s. Family time turned into the *Jeopardy* game show, except that we didn't win any money and Dad got to pick the categories: French Huguenot history for 200. Invertebrate biology for 300.

"Dad, I have no idea," I said in response to one of his trivia questions. "You *know* I don't know. Cut me a break."

My father's most notorious family time activities weren't

academic or literary; they were spiritual. He would ask us questions like, "How did you see the presence of God in your day today?" Or, as a way to bring together humor, metaphor, and my mother's dinner menu, he would ask, "How is the Christian life like a plate full of spaghetti?" My brothers and I had to ponder the analogy—maybe grace is a good meatball?—and then after a while, one of us would hold up our shackled wrists and ask to be excused.

My mother too had intense parenting tics. As an ex-hippy who didn't want her kids to end up brainwashed by mainstream America, she initiated a loosely mandated ban against instruments of pop and consumer culture. On her list of taboos:

TV = lazy bones

Video games = bad reader

Headphones = bad listener

Sunglasses = bad eye contact

"You can't trust a person who hides his eyes," she would say. "You look a person right in the eye; that's what you do."

My parents never bought a TV. Instead of watching cartoons, we read comic books, kids books, and biographies of Christian history. My mother read us stories about Amy Carmichael, the missionary to India, and George Washington Carver, the African-American botanist who in the 1920s helped alleviate poverty in the South. After dinner every night, my parents took turns reading aloud to the whole family from books like the Lord of the Rings series and the Narnia series.

Along with the taboos and the TV alternatives, my parents developed an arsenal of Christian character-forming mantras that were meant to counter the excesses of Western individualism (like selfishness) and teach us how to be strong, brave, and good.

Mantra 1: "Love is a choice, not a feeling."

This phrase was meant to help us overcome the weak, bleeding-heart melodrama of teen and preteen behavior. Before I was even old enough to have a crush on the kid next door, I knew love and marriage were not about romance but about choice, commitment, and endurance. Heavy stuff for a ten-year-old. I tease my parents now for laying on their kids such crushing truths of life, but they were honest, at least, doing their best to abolish the delusions of childhood.

Mantra 2: "Happiness is a choice."

As a sibling mantra to "Love is a choice," this phrase meant "Quit your bellyaching. Check your attitude."

Mantra 3: "It's good missionary training."

My parents used this phrase when my brothers and I complained about doing things we didn't like. It became the catch-all call for "Buck up and deal with it" and sometimes involved leaning over our dinner plates to shovel in the beans that we didn't want to eat.

Mantra 4: "Choices have consequences."

This phrase usually came before a spank to the backside and was another way of saying, "You chose this, not me. Try door number two next time."

Mantra 5: "Go M.A.D."

M.A.D. was an acronym for "make a difference." After

hearing the phrase from Christian radio host Ron Hutch-craft, my mother started using it every day as my brothers and I walked out the door to catch the school bus. Kids, not just adults, were responsible to help alleviate the burden of the human condition by making the world a better place to live.

Going M.A.D. took various forms. When I was eight, my parents signed up to be foster parents with a humanitarian organization called Healing the Children, which brought patients from all over the world for medical treatment in the US. My brothers and I became temporary siblings to kids with brittle bone disease and Down syndrome who came for months or sometimes years to live with us. We pushed them around in their wheelchairs, played with them, and shared our bedrooms with them.

As if being a foster family wasn't enough, after school once a week my mom took us to visit elderly widows from the church who were cooped up at home watching TV and reading large-print copies of *Reader's Digest.* "You're ambassadors for the family," my mother said as we walked up to the front door of a widow's house. That was another one of her parenting mantras. In other words: Be good. Do good.

In so many ways, it humors me to remember the intensity of how I was raised. As the architects of my childhood, my parents mixed hippy social-justice values and Christian values to reinforce one overarching principle: anything that distracts you from a fierce focus on God, meaning, and the amelioration of suffering is not worth a cat sniff. Life was all about the big stuff—reaping wisdom from epic allegories like *The Pilgrim's Progress* and saving girls from sex exploitation.

Even now, I can still picture my mom holding up books at the dining room table and reading to us from those stories of hope and humanity. I can still remember my father saying in so many words to a hitchhiker, "Your name means something. Your life means something too." A Christian, moral, and philanthropic imperative motivated my mom and dad. It drove them as parents. It also drove them in their decision to go to Africa as missionaries.

■ ■ ■

When my parents were first married back in the early '70s, they spent five years in Tucson while my dad did his internal medicine residency at the University of Arizona. At a church potluck sometime at the end of his residency, my parents heard about a Quaker organization called Friends United Meeting that was looking for medical missionary volunteers. My parents applied and then accepted an invitation to go to Africa. In July of 1979, we flew to England so my dad could attend tropical medicine school for three months. Then we moved to East Africa, where we lived for almost six years.

The Quakers commissioned my parents to the Lugulu Friends Hospital in a rural agrarian area of western Kenya. The town of Lugulu had a quarter-mile strip of *dukas*, small storefronts made of mud thatch with corrugated tin pinned down for roofs. In the farm fields outside town, women worked by hand with their babies tied on their backs, tilling their way across the wide countryside of the western highlands. It was an eight-hour drive from Lugulu to Nairobi.

International mail took weeks and often months to reach us. Phone calls cost a fortune. We lived out in the bush, as people called it. The US was so far away that in 1981 when we got a package from Uncle John in Chicago containing an audiocassette of the ethereal music to *Chariots of Fire*, my parents thought the film was about aliens.

The story of my parents' first year as missionaries is part of family lore. When we first arrived, Ben at age five learned from his new Kenyan friends how to swear in Bukusu, the local tribal language. One of the neighbors came to my mother and said, "Do you know what your son's saying?" My mom was appalled. Ben was sitting at the top of a guava tree cussing. Not long afterward, he threw a stick at our next-door neighbor, a woman named Florah. Throwing sticks at the neighbor doesn't usually come recommended in the manual on how to start missionary life. Swearing from the top of a tree doesn't come recommended either.

As the child of my missionary parents, I have my own memories, one of which is captured in a photograph that I've kept all these years. My brothers and I are sitting with our dad in a dead baobab tree. We're crouched together in the heart of the tree where the branches depart from the trunk, looking small in the great expanse around us and yet safe in our father's arms. The picture is framed in a wide panorama. Mount Kilimanjaro rises behind us. The Rift Valley savanna spreads out to the east and west, part of a three-thousand-mile basin that cuts a long swathe from Syria all the way south to Mozambique.

Historically, the Rift is purported to be the origin of all humanity. To me, it represents the origin of my childhood not just geographically—I grew up on the high plains that run west of the Rift—but spiritually. I came to faith in that place. The trajectory of my spiritual history began there. My relationship with the church began there too.

Every Sunday in Lugulu, we attended a nondenominational church that met in an A-frame auditorium. I liked church as a kid. For most of the service, we stood singing, almost seven hundred people clapping and shaking our tambourines as mourning doves hovered and cooed in the rafters above. The auditorium had tall windows that were almost always left open. Walking across the compound toward the church, you could hear the sound of the congregation swelling and lifting in song. I've never heard anything like it again.

As a multilingual church, we sang both in English and in Swahili. One of the hymns was called "Mungu Yu Mwema":

Mungu yu mwema (God is so good),
Mungu yu mwema (God is so good),
Mungu yu mwema (God is so good),
Yu mwema kwangu (He is so good to me).

That hymn reminds me of my childhood in Kenya the way sugar cane and hibiscus flowers remind me of that time. It conjures up, too, a whole community of people who raised me to believe in God and in God's goodness.

Over the fence behind our house lived Florah Ashene, the woman Ben threw a stick at when we first arrived. She taught home economics at the local high school and took part in a weekly Bible study with my parents and other neighbors in Lugulu. All the kids in the study memorized

35

Bible verses and then recited them to parents in the fellow-ship. When it was Florah's turn to be my "Scripture auntie," I walked over to her house, stood in her kitchen, and said my passage by heart. She hugged me and sent me home with bananas.

Down the road lived Elijah Malenji, a man who became like an uncle to the kids in the community. He loved on us and prayed for us. As an evangelist with Trinity Fellow-ship, he owned an old reel-to-reel film projector and used to show Christian films like *The Pilgrim's Progress* at the high school auditorium where we met for church or on the hospital wards where my dad worked. We watched the '70s version with bad actors wearing fake, pointy beards and black Puritan hats. I remember sitting in the dark on the hospital's cold cement floor, listening to the sound of filmstrip ticking through the film reel as moths crossed the projector beam and Pilgrim trudged through the Slough of Despond.

Next door to us lived a Ugandan refugee named Betsy Kamuka, who worked with my dad at the hospital as head nurse and director of the medical student program. She was a smart, tough woman whose husband had left her to raise their son, Ivan, alone. We called her "Auntie Betsy." If other people in Lugulu were like backup singers for my spiritual formation, then Auntie Betsy was the lead gospel singer. She was the one who led me to faith. I was converted to Christianity not by my religious parents, strangely, but by an African Christian living in Lugulu.

On the day of my conversion, I had gone over to Betsy's house to cook with her, something I did often. Her kitchen was the size of a closet with a small window facing south into the sun. That afternoon, while she and I sat beside a Kenyan jiko stove stirring a pot of frying onions, she asked me questions in the style of an informal catechism.

Do you know that God made you and loves you?

Do you believe that Jesus died for your sins?

Do you want to follow Jesus?

I don't remember what I said, exactly. But I remember insignificant details, those fragmented snapshots of a child's memory, like the can of Blue Band margarine sitting on the ground beside us as we talked and cooked. I remember, too, the feel of the cold iron frame of Betsy's bed after she invited me back into her room to ask Jesus into my heart. I held onto it while kneeling down in the dim light and leaning my head against the mattress to pray. There was no fanfare and no emotional frenzy. The experience seemed almost matter-of-fact. In the Lugulu community, learning about God was tantamount to learning about gravity. You had to understand it to make sense of things. Simple as that. After we prayed, Betsy said "Amen," and then we went back to her kitchen to cook.

As I look back now, I see my child self as another person, the kid I once was kneeling by a bed and making a significant existential decision. I'm not sure I had full awareness of what it meant. But what stands out more than the moment of my conversion are the years surrounding it, the larger religious context that set the course for the rest of my life. I grew up in a cross-cultural Christian community driven by an intense sense of ultimate purpose. Everything mattered. Every person mattered. Every moment mattered.

As a kid, I felt carried by the stability of that community and by the strength of its purpose. I remember many evenings falling asleep on my mother's lap in a living room full of neighbors. Listening at first to conversation about East African politics or child rearing or church building, I would slip into a state of oblivion as their voices became a soft, collective murmur carrying me into the night, like ocean waves taking me out on the tide. The adults made sense of the world while I drifted off to sleep.

■ ■ ■

Not everything, though, seemed harbored to safety in the hands of a good community and a good God. Six months before we arrived in Africa and one year after I was born, Uganda's dictator Idi Amin went into exile and left behind one of the century's most horrific genocides, a reign of darkness and bloodletting that threw its shadow over all of East Africa and over the community of Lugulu. Located only hours from the Ugandan border, Lugulu was flooded with refugees who lived through Amin's regime. They were doctors and nurses at the hospital where my dad worked, teachers at the nearby high school, kids next door. Down the road from us lived a family who had fled Amin's soldiers, forded a river with their five children, the youngest ones riding piggyback, and found shelter in a room behind a bar just inside the Kenyan border.

I grew up in this setting. Mortality and instability were almost mundane. On any given day in Lugulu, my dad was diagnosing sickle-cell at the hospital. My mom was praying the last prayer on someone's deathbed and then pinching ants off her son's pants after he'd climbed an infested hibiscus tree in the front yard. When the Kenyan military tried to overthrow the president, I overheard my parents talking with neighbors about *coup d'état*, and when Obote took over Uganda after Amin, I heard them talk about guerilla armies. I pictured men crouched in the back of army trucks, passing under trees where black, hairy gorillas waited to leap down and ambush them in the dark.

Rather than shelter their kids, my mom and dad brought us alongside. Although I didn't know it at the time, that decision had a lot to do with how my faith was formed. My parents said in so many words, Hey, this is the way it is. This is life in the world you live in. Sometimes things get messy. Sometimes God's a mystery. My dad, for example, took my older brother to Uganda during government unrest. During drought, we hauled water from the cistern along with our neighbors. We attended funerals for my dad's patients and helped paint the casket for a stillborn baby. When my mom visited people on the hospital wards every week, my brothers and I went with her.

While most American kids my age were playing Pac-Man or watching cartoons, I was spending time in a rural Quaker hospital in western Kenya. To this day, I can still picture the inpatient wards and the white-smocked nurses scurrying around the stations at the far end of the room. I can see the worn iron bed frames lined up in symmetrical rows, the gray wool blankets on each bed, the cold cement floors. I remember what it was like walking into the ward every week and being overwhelmed by the stench of urine and antiseptic. We learned how to pinch our noses and breathe through our mouths. On every visit, my mom and I sat next to one hospital bed after another. We talked with each patient. We prayed with them and brought them books to read. To the kids on the ward, we brought our basket of Legos.

On one of our hospital rounds, we met a twelve-year-old boy named Losokwoi. He had come from the nomadic Pokot tribe in northern Kenya to be treated for severe tuberculosis of the brain and weighed about forty pounds from malnourishment. The nurses flipped him from side to side, trying to take care of his constant bedsores. He couldn't walk. He couldn't speak Swahili. But every week, Ben played Legos with him, spreading the pieces out on the blanket in between Losokwoi's legs.

Losokwoi stayed in Lugulu for about two months. It was long enough for us to get to know him well. Somewhere toward the end of that time, the missionary pastor who had come with him to Lugulu baptized him in our bathroom tub. One afternoon, my dad brought Losokwoi from the hospital and pushed his wheelchair through our living room and down the hallway to the bathroom. Then he and the pastor together lifted the boy's frail body out of the chair and lowered him into the tub. I stood out in the hallway with my mom and brothers, watching as the pastor bent him back into the tub water in the name of the Father, the Son, and the Holy Spirit, amen.

Losokwoi died two weeks later. My father came home from the hospital one morning before the sun rose and told us. "The nurses haven't removed his body from the ward," he said to my mother. "None of the night staff want to go to the morgue. They're leaving it for a day worker. But I don't want to wait. I need Ben."

My mom consented, and I watched my nine-year-old brother head out in the early morning dark to go see his dead friend — one boy preparing another boy for burial. My dad carried the body, and Ben carried the keys. They walked from the hospital to the morgue, a mud hut building that sat forty feet from the front door of our house. My brother waited outside while my father went in and laid Losokwoi's body in the morgue. They came home just as the sun was beginning to rise.

As we sat at the dining room table that morning, my dad bowed his head to say a blessing. Halfway through the prayer, he covered his face with his hands and started sobbing. We had guests visiting from Scandinavia. Everyone sat quietly for a moment, wondering what to do with a grown man and his grief. Then my mom took over saying the prayer. I kept my eyes open the whole time, watching my dad weep with a kind of transparency that shocked me. I had never seen him cry before.

Two days later, my mom drove my brothers and me to the funeral in a small town called Kitale. Dad couldn't go; he had to stay and work at the hospital. During the ceremony, we stood by the hole and helped throw dirt onto the wood coffin. A small frog jumped in. A pastor said a prayer. Some kids stood up and sang a song called "Jesus, I Heard You Have a Big House" as cemetery workers shoveled the remaining dirt.

Driving home, my mom talked to us about death.

"Losokwoi's body is like a tent that he lived in here on earth," she said. "Just like in camping, he's done with his tent now. It's been folded up and put away. But the real Losokwoi is with Jesus in heaven." We were riding in the old '67 Ford Escort that we inherited as the Quaker missionary family. Along with my brothers, I sat on the ripped leather seats in the back and watched trees pass by outside the windows. None of us said anything.

Right then, all I knew was that a little boy had died and that I felt upset by it in a strange, inarticulate way. Years later, though, Losokwoi's death meant something more to me. It became part of my pilgrim burden, one of those small stones in my heart that I carried around for years before I felt its full weight and before it gave heft to my struggle with the so-called problem of evil. Something was profoundly wrong with the world. God allowed suffering. God let a good kid die.

Chapter 2

DARTH VADER
LOVES JESUS

Kathy Crosby

Vacation Bible school, 1986

For Halloween in third grade, I dressed up as Amy Carmichael. My mother found some white linen fabric and, using safety pins to hold it together, fashioned an Indian sari. I wore the sari to school with a pair of pink moon boots. Walking down the halls in a throng of witches and goblins, I ran into a student who looked at my rumpled white sari and said, "What are you, a mummy?"

"I'm not a mummy," I said indignantly. "I'm a missionary!"

I was fresh out of the mission field and a total misfit. After six years in Kenya, our family had moved to Spokane, Washington, where my dad started teaching in an internal medicine residency program affiliated with the University of Washington. Situated in the foothills of the Rocky Mountains three hundred miles from the Pacific Ocean, eastern Washington looked entirely different from western Kenya. Instead of open country, I looked out at mountains and pines. There wasn't a guava tree in sight.

The landscape of public school seemed just as foreign. My classmates didn't know what to do with me. While they were pegging their stretch pants like MC Hammer and listening to New Kids on the Block, I was dressing up as a sex-slave-liberating missionary from the 1930s. My regular clothing, too, went over as well as my Halloween costume. I wore the same outfit for days in succession — not something you do in America, my peers told me. You buy clothes. Lots of clothes. You also go to movies like E.T. For years after watching that film, I had nightmares in which E.T. staggered toward me out of a half-lit cornfield, moaning.

Even mundane experiences jarred me. The first time I went over to some friends' house to play, I opened the fridge to look for a snack and saw a cold Corona beer sitting in the back corner of the shelf behind a gallon of milk. The beer belonged to the kids' dad, Scott. As soon as I saw it, my heart seized up with moral horror. I thought to myself, Scott is going to hell. Those exact words went through my head. To a kid coming from the conservative, prohibitionist Christianity of East Africa, beer came "from the devil." I adopted that cultural taboo as a child and watched my parents adopt

44

it too. Even after moving back to the States, I never saw my parents drink a lick of alcohol while I was a kid. They didn't even take wine. To me, Scott was a total heathen.

I laugh about that story now, but back then it was part of a disorienting assimilation process. I felt the way a cat might feel if it were swept into a crate, driven two hundred miles, and then let out at a strange house. Everything about my new life seemed foreign. In that transition, I became what's called a "third-culture kid," someone who spends significant time in another country, blends the birthplace culture and the new culture into a "third culture," and never quite feels at ease in her own country. Home is always somewhere else.

Eventually, I learned how to fit in with my American peers and how to watch adults drink beer without passing them off as eternally damned. It took time. My parents helped with the transition. They took us to the state fair to ride a Ferris wheel for the first time. They took us camping and taught us the names of new trees. They also started taking us to an old Presbyterian church called Knox. As the second church of my upbringing, that community played as significant a part in my American childhood as the Lugulu community did my Kenyan childhood.

The head pastor at Knox ran a T-shirt business, sat on the city council, and preached in the pulpit every Sunday. In the summers, he hosted big church potlucks at the park near his house. We barbecued hot dogs and ate green Jell-O with marshmallows, a dish made by the church matriarchs that to this day I associate with growing up Presbyterian. Often on Saturday nights, I slept over at the pastor's house with his two daughters. We stayed up late watching movies and sitting on high stools in the third floor bathroom while the pastor's wife rolled pink sponge curlers into our hair for church the next day.

The pastor's kids and others became my church playmates, the friends I associate with Knox in the same way that I associate my Kenyan and Ugandan friends with Lugulu. Instead of running around a rural hospital compound, we ran around an old church in a low-income neighborhood of central Spokane. The building's mismatched brick gave it a shabby appearance. Across the street sat a meth house that eventually burned to the ground. Two blocks away was a low-income apartment building that also went up in flames one day.

Flanked on all sides by streets and alleyways, the church had almost no yard. The interior of the church, not the exterior, became our open country. I don't remember much about attending services or Sunday school. But I remember the interstices, the in-between time spent roaming inside the church with other "Knox kids." While our parents stood in the fellowship hall sipping coffee and talking about Thessalonians next to a painting of Christ, my friends and I sneaked into the church kitchen to stick our licked fingers into the giant can of Kool-Aid powder and then went darting between the tables, taking lemon bars from the coffee-hour spread.

More than coffee-hour tag or Kool-Aid raids, vacation Bible school stands out in my memory as the apex of my childhood at Knox. Every summer, the head pastor, Joel, directed an internship program that drew college students

46

from all over the West Coast to work with our church youth. The interns became idols to us, cool college kids who came to hang out with us for June, July, and August. They took us to camp, led youth group, and directed VBS as if it were Woodstock for kids, with less weed and more Jesus.

I looked forward to VBS like some kids look forward to the circus. Five days a week for three hours a day, I spent time going from room to room for craft lessons, Bible lessons, and games in the gym. I ate sticky orange popsicles in the church kitchen as a reward for memorizing verses and watched older kids dunk our pastors in the dunk tank out on the front lawn. What kid doesn't want to watch her church preacher get dropped into a water tank? VBS was like a carnival of morally acceptable indulgences.

At the very end of each day, all the kids from different grades got together and watched a theater performance put on in the sanctuary by the college interns and the church staff. Each skit series had a catchy theme. For the first VBS I ever attended after coming back from Kenya, the pastors had picked a superhero theme. Entering the sanctuary, I noticed that the pews in the choir loft had been moved back. Underneath the wooden cross and behind the pulpit sat a giant eight-foot-high Bible made of cardboard and marked in capital letters "LIVING BIBLE." Interns came and went from the stage carrying secret costumes and stage props.

After the pews had filled, the kids started yelling and clapping, summoning the characters onto stage. In choreographed appearance, Batman and Robin came running down the center aisle. Wonder Woman jumped out on the stage. Robin leapt up the stairs to the LIVING BIBLE and said, turning to his partner, "Holy Scripture, Batman!"

I still love that line. I don't know who wrote the skits, but they were schmaltzy in the best way. Wonder Woman joined Batman and Robin and together they opened the Bible and read the verse of the day out loud—"I can do all things through Christ who strengthens me"—just in time for the two bad guys to come pouncing out on stage to thwart our heroes' do-gooder plot. The villains that week included Darth Vader from *Star Wars* and Dr. Doom from *The Fantastic Four* (wearing oven mitts for hands and a green-sheet cape).

While Batman and Robin clashed with Doom on the church stage, at the base of the stairs, Wonder Woman did faux karate kicks on Darth Vader while trying to soften his mean heart. "Stop fighting it, Vader! Jesus loves you!" Batman got distracted fixing his cape—all part of the script—while Dr. Doom kidnapped Robin and threw him over his shoulder, bounding down the center aisle in a show of diabolical power. (Lesson: overcoming evil isn't easy.)

Suddenly, Spiderman appeared overhead in the balcony as the surprise superhero towering above us on the banister our parents had warned us never to stand on. "Not so quick, Dr. Doom," he said. We shrieked and gasped as Spiderman leapt off the banister in a staged act that went wrong when his blue leotard snagged on the balcony nail that held the Christmas wreath every year. He stole the show that morning when he came crashing into the center aisle, surrounded by more than two hundred cheering kids.

All of the skit characters seemed like sidekicks for Action Figure Jesus. We loved it. Sometimes at the end of a performance, the characters froze in place onstage and

Pastor Joel would get up and ask the kids in the audience something like, "What does Darth Vader need?"

"Jesus!"

By the end of the week, the bad guys accepted Christ and the heroes forgave the villains. Darth Vader took off his mask after being saved. So did Dr. Doom. Evil threatened good. Then evil converted to good.

To the kids in the pews, VBS meant fun and games. But to the parents and the pastors, VBS was all about spiritual formation. Everything happened for a higher purpose. Pop culture was appropriated for Jesus. Levity served sobriety. Comic book heroes pointed to the divine. The pastors wanted to teach us about faith. They knew having fun was part of being a kid, so they translated biblical principles into an attractive story we could understand, in the way cathedrals in the Middle Ages used stained-glass windows to illustrate the gospel narratives for an illiterate population. VBS made theology visual, simple, and unambiguous.

As I got older, the pastors put the same spiritual structure around youth group. Every week after playing a game of dodge ball in the gym and knocking each other down with half-deflated rubber balls, the Knox kids sat down with youth leaders for serious dialogue about faith. We talked about materialism and humanism. We talked about factions within Christianity, the free-willers versus the Calvinists. We learned about how God was the Creator of the universe, the universe had a beginning, and the consciousness of God existed in some form in every society as "eternity set in the heart of man." I still have some of the lesson handouts, which referenced Scripture, history, and literature.

49

Following discussion time, we planned our next mission project—painting a church in a rural part of Washington State, building a house in Mexico, or doing yard work for the neighbors who lived around Knox. Before any mission, our youth group leaders and other adults in the church— including my mother—gave lessons on how to be a "host" (a giver) rather than a "guest" (a taker) and on how to have an "attitude of gratitude" in every situation. The leaders used phrases at church the way my parents used mantras at home. As memorable aphorisms meant to evoke Christian purpose and moral character, these phrases became part of the high roof over my head and part of what I remember so vividly about my early faith formation.

What I remember most clearly about those years at Knox is being raised in the company of really good-hearted people. They made our family feel at home after coming back from Kenya. They took meat loaf to firefighters when eastern Washington went up in flames one year. They volunteered on the PTA, ran canned food drives, and helped raise each other's kids in community. Every Sunday, they gathered together at church the way we used to gather in the auditorium in Kenya, hundreds of people singing "How Great Thou Art" as morning light filtered through the stained-glass windows of the sanctuary.

■ ■ ■

When I was twelve years old, my little brother and I were baptized in this church community. In the months leading up to the service, my mother picked us up from elementary school and dropped us off at church for baptismal preparation. Nathan met with Joel, the head pastor. I met with Van, the youth pastor. Van had played Darth Vader in the VBS skits. We thought he was the coolest thing since push-up popsicles. He wore a black leather jacket, rode a motorcycle, and parked his motorcycle in the pastor's parking spot.

During our sessions, Van discussed with me the significance of baptism. What did it mean, exactly, and was I ready? As evangelical Presbyterians, we practiced baptism as a public declaration of what happened privately in the heart at conversion. It marked a theological coming-of-age. For me, it marked the second and probably more significant milestone in my coming to faith.

Sitting forward with his long legs crossed, Van during one session asked me three questions in the style of a catechism, not unlike the way Betsy Kamuka in Kenya had asked me questions in her kitchen.

Van said, "Do you believe in Jesus as your Lord and Savior?"

"Yes," I said.

"Do you desire to honor him with your life, by following his ways?"

"Yes."

"Will you be a part of his church?"

"Yes."

I answered these questions with guilelessness and sincerity. No one had pressured me to get baptized. I answered for myself and by myself. Along with the baptism that followed, that exchange with Van was possibly the last time in a long time that I would feel total clarity of belief.

On the day of the baptism, cars lined both sides of our street. Nathan and I had decided that we wanted the event to take place in the river in our back yard. The Little Spokane River, which came out of the foothills of the Rocky Mountains, went bending in an S-curve past our property. When we told our friends in Kenya that we had bought a house by a small river, they were so pleased. We had easy access to clean drinking water. We wouldn't have to walk far to fill our buckets. Drought wouldn't be an issue for us.

That Saturday afternoon, our family and friends gathered on the south bank of the river. The sun was out. It was late summer. Joel and Van stood in their Hawaiian swimming trunks and flip flops, sharing about the meaning of baptism and holding open Bibles in their hands while the high midday sun flashed on the river current behind them.

After the pastors spoke, they invited people to share words of wisdom. A family friend from our church gave Nathan a deck of baseball cards and talked about how faith grows in value the way cards grow in value over time. His wife gave me a Chinese paper butterfly to signify rebirth. We sang a hymn, standing in small groups reading the lyrics off photocopies my mother made at the church office. Then Van handed off his Bible and stepped into the water.

"Baptism is a sacrament in the Presbyterian Church," he said, turning to the people standing on the riverbank. "By choosing to be baptized, we are casting our lot with Jesus Christ and making a public profession of faith."

Turning back to me and putting his left arm around my shoulder, he said, "Andrea Palpant, do you place your trust in Jesus Christ?" I listened to Van as if he were a father, not just a pastor. He seemed wise and calm.

"I do."

"Do you desire to follow him?"

"I do."

The current pushed against my legs with force, separating at my waist and reconverging behind me like floodwaters moving around a rock. Van held me steady. Then in the name of the Father, the Son, and the Holy Spirit, he braced my back with his long arm and took me under. I went bending beneath the surface of the river, closing my eyes and holding my breath in the dark undercurrent.

After Van pulled me out, he prayed the closing prayer and said my full name again in a way that made me feel as if God himself had said my name. In that moment, I felt the blessing of a priest upon me. The feeling of being known and understood. The feeling of belonging to God's great cosmos.

Chapter 3

WHY ISN'T GOD LIKE ERIC CLAPTON?

In seventh grade, my English teacher required us to bring in our own book for free reading time. I chose a paperback from my parents' bookshelf. The title appeared in bold, embossed letters on the cover: *Disappointment with God* by Philip Yancey. I remember my teacher leaning over my desk with her eyebrow raised at the book I'd brought to school with me.

"What's that about?" she asked.

I don't remember what I said. Probably something about the Israelites living in exile in the wilderness. To her, the book no doubt seemed like an odd, precocious choice for a junior high student. That kind of literature was read by faith-weary fortysomethings, not thirteen-year-olds. But to me, *Disappointment with God* seemed like a perfectly natural book to pick up. As a teenager undergoing what psychologists might call "spiritual individuation," I wanted to figure out what I believed. And how else do you talk about faith but in terms of doubt and disappointment?

I was being raised in a church community by the same good people who taught me Sunday school and came to my birthday parties and stood at my baptism in Christian love. But love is never enough. When you tip over the steep edge of childhood and plummet into puberty, you grow big feet. Everything about you becomes awkward, including your heart.

My Sunday school teachers can tell you what happened to me at that age. I started asking questions. Questions I knew they couldn't answer easily. Questions that people had been wrestling with in much more sophisticated forms for centuries. Every Sunday, I went to class in a third-floor room lined with ratty couches like those you might find in the basement of a college dormitory. Sunk back into a couch cushion, I would raise my skinny arm to demand all sorts of impossible answers to impossible questions. I wanted to know:

> If God is real, why don't my friends at school know about him?
>
> Why doesn't God talk the way he talked to Moses — from burning bushes?
>
> Why is there so much war in the Old Testament?
>
> Why did Jesus show up with a body just once in all of history?
>
> Why is there a homeless man standing on the corner in the cold?
>
> Why do little boys die of tuberculosis?

The questions didn't come out of nowhere. They came from growing up in Kenya. They came, too, from my experiences on mission trips, serving cooking lard and corn to refugees and helping to build a one-room house for a homeless family. After a while, I started wondering. What's going on here? Who's running the show? Every time I saw suffering of any kind, I felt a stone drop into my heart. Losokwoi was a stone. Homeless hungry people were a stone. Refugees were a stone. Collectively, they became the burden I hauled around in my growing disappointment with God.

Not unlike most teenagers undergoing their first spiritual or emotional crisis, I found solace and escape in music. In particular, the shift in my musical interests reflected the shift going on in my heart. I went from church hymns like "How Great Thou Art" to the songs of drug-addled '80s bands. The transition happened over a period of years.

When I was in junior high and he was in high school, Ben started tracking all the current music in the contemporary Christian scene. I followed Ben's taste. We listened to Michael W. Smith and Amy Grant. We listened to Carman, the "Italian Stallion" who greased his hair back and looked like a mafia-hit-man-turned-pastor. We listened to Code of Ethics, an electronica group whose music sounded like that of any early '90s band but with a "higher power" theme tacked on. We bought tickets, too, for Christian rock concerts and stood in the metal bleachers of the high school gym getting our adrenaline digs to Christian songs like "Addicted to Jesus," "Hand of Providence," and "Radically Saved."

Everything changed a few years later. Ben went off to college at a Quaker liberal arts school in Oregon and moved into a dorm room with someone who liked to listen to Brit pop and other mainstream music. Shortly after, Ben started sending me cassette tapes.

"It's from your brother," my mother said one night while cutting an onion for dinner. She pointed to a padded manila envelope on the counter. I opened the package and found a tape along with a short note written on a torn piece of notebook paper. "My roommate Hans," Ben wrote, "has all this great music. I hope you like it." Scanning the tape's cover insert, I saw the names of song titles and musicians I didn't recognize: Depeche Mode, U2, Erasure. The tape was labeled *The Secular Collection.*

As a child growing up with an evangelical vocabulary, I had the impression that *secular* was a bad word. Its synonym, *worldly,* was another bad word. Our church didn't follow a strict separation from American pop culture; we learned about God via superheroes. As a kid, though, I tended to see the world in more black-and-white terms than did the adults around me. To me, the difference between Christian and secular cultures seemed as obvious as the difference between a healthy meal and a shelf-baked Twinkie: one tasted better but rotted out your insides. The other one had vitamin longevity. That Christian-secular divide ran straight through the territory of music. When he left for college, Ben crossed the divide and carried me with him.

After opening the package at the kitchen counter that evening, I took a drive in the Plymouth hatchback that still belonged to Ben and had the Ichthus stuck on the back bumper. I had just gotten my driver's license. With no particular destination in mind, I climbed into the car, buckled my seat belt, and slip-popped *The Secular Collection* into the car's temperamental tape player. The deck didn't intake a tape; it *swallowed* it like a chunk of plastic, and you never knew if the cassette would play or get chewed up like string cheese.

One of the first tracks I heard—"Higher Love" by Depeche Mode—seemed like a song a person might listen to while running alone at night. The melody was minor-key, gloomy, and beautiful. The lyrics, though, sounded vague and slightly affected:

> I can taste more than feel
> This burning inside is so real
> Moved, lifted higher
> Moved, my soul's on fire
> Moved, by a higher love

Who knows what the lead singer Dave Gahan was trying to say. Maybe the song was a post-Christian plea for God by a British musician who was once declared clinically dead from drug overdose in his Los Angeles hotel room before paramedics revived him. Maybe it was just a cry for higher purpose. For me, listening to his minor key dirge made me want to brood and smoke out on the back porch in that cliché, coming-of-age kind of way. It also afflicted me with genuine discontent.

After *The Secular Collection*, Ben sent me other tapes. He labeled each one with his meticulous handwriting, listing the artists and song titles and album names. Every evening, I set up a cheap tape player on my bedroom desk and listened to those cassettes. I was the diligent high school student doing her homework to music from "the other side."

To anyone who didn't grow up in a semiprotected religious environment, all of this will seem almost comical or melodramatic. I started listening to non-Christian music. Big deal. But that's the point. To me it *was* a big deal. Now, as an adult, I see the tension between sacred (or Christian) art and secular art as a mostly false dichotomy. Back then, that dichotomy seemed very real. It meant something to me. On one side I saw church, hymns, and my parents. On the other side I saw angst, doubt, and Depeche Mode.

In search of answers, I started going to people in my life who knew something— *anything*—about that "other side." Ben, of course, was one of them. An old family friend named Scott Edminster was one of them too. I knew from spending time at his house with his kids that Scott listened to mainstream music on the radio stations. In my mind, that meant he knew something about what I'd come to see as the threshold— the space between the church and everything beyond the church. I thought he might have something to say about my search.

I asked him about it once, while riding in his pickup truck one afternoon. I was sixteen years old. We were on our way to the Edminsters' cabin. The rest of the family followed in a van. Crossing over the Rocky Mountains and dropping down into the plains of western Montana, we talked for three hours and listened to old Dire Straits songs on the car stereo. Scott loved Woodstock-era rock. He also loved wrestling. All four of his sons wrestled on the high school team, and when the song "Money for Nothing" came on, Scott said, "This would be a great song to open with at a wrestling match, don't you think?"

"Yeah, that would be awesome."

"When all the wrestlers come running around the mat in a circle—do you know what I'm talking about?"

"Yeah, that's perfect. It's got adrenaline."

"I'll tell Coach Stone."

"Scott," I said, changing the topic suddenly. "Doesn't faith feel mythical to you?"

Being with Scott was like spending time with an old family priest. He'd known me from the day I was born but didn't set my curfew. He was a father figure and a friend, a man's man and an ER doctor who after volunteering with Russian patients at a low-income clinic started calling me "Andreavich" in his avuncular way. Gritty, smart, and tough, he was the kind of man who read Tolstoy's *The Death of Ivan Ilyich* on his back deck and then went out to the garage to chop wood for the winter. He was also the family friend whose Corona beer I'd found in the fridge and taken as a sign of his eternal damnation. Now that I was a teenager walking the outer edge of faith, Scott represented the possibility of reasoned and confident belief.

After my question, Scott paused and then spoke. "Money for Nothing" was still playing in the background. He said to me, "You know, Andrea, myth in principle isn't a bad thing. Myth is just a way of making sense out of the world based on what we know and see. It's how we put structure around things."

I nodded.

"I don't mean that faith is a myth. I mean that stories sometimes communicate truth better than facts do."

"How can you be certain about faith?"

"I'm *not* certain about anything. But for me, Christianity is where I, like Pascal, want to lay my wager. It's where my hope lies. It's the only compelling vision."

"But doesn't atheism seem more believable?"

"Atheism doesn't have definitive proof any more than Christianity does. My study of the remarkable human body alone would cause me to say quite confidently that it takes more faith to be an atheist than it does to be a theist."

"I guess so," I said halfheartedly.

"For me, these mountains are proof enough that there's a creative God."

By then, we had arrived in the small town of Yaak, Montana. Out the window, I saw dilapidated barns, rusted machinery, and miles of woods and wilderness. As Scott turned off the main highway past the Dirty Shame Saloon and drove down a long dirt road, our conversation drifted to other topics. I didn't feel the kind of resolution that I wanted. But then, everywhere I turned, answers seemed hard to come by. No one could tell me what I wanted to hear—that the world wasn't as screwed up as it seemed, and that God the Cosmic Office Manager was just taking a shift break in a galaxy bathroom and would be out in a moment to make the universe right.

Even the books I read told a different and more depressing story. Some of them were books I read in high school. One morning, my English teacher stood up, clapped her hands, and said, "Today, everyone, you're going to learn about existentialism." Over weeks and months, we read books like *The Stranger* and *The Plague* by Albert Camus.

We read classic works of American literature, too, like *The Grapes of Wrath* by John Steinbeck and *Death of a Salesman* by Arthur Miller. According to Miller, life was tough and mean and hard on the soul. People lost hope. Men killed themselves. Sons went fatherless.

On the day we finished reading *Death of a Salesman*, I went and stood by my teacher's desk.

"What am I supposed to do with this?" I asked her. "It's so dark. There's no relief, none at all."

"I know," she said. "I know."

"I've never felt like this after reading a book."

"You're not the first."

"It feels so bitter and godless. What am I supposed to do?"

■ ■ ■

My English teacher and Scott Edminster were not the only adults in whom I confided about my doubt. My dad played a role in my faith journey too.

Back in 1967, my dad was a premed student at Penn State University going through a skeptic phase. One afternoon, he was sitting in the student union building studying biology when a student evangelist approached him, carrying a Christian tract called *The Four Spiritual Laws*. As my dad listened to the evangelist present his message, my dad pretended not to believe. He played the antagonistic agnostic and asked all sorts of difficult philosophical questions, leaving the student stymied and confused.

"I never did tell him I was a Christian," my dad said when

he told the story. As kids, we loved this story in the same way some kids admire their parents for the edgy, sexy stuff they did when they were young, like skydiving or smoking pot. I saw my dad as *bad*, back when *bad* meant "cool," just for giving some over-eager Christian a hard time.

Between my parents' engagement in 1969 and their marriage a year later, my dad's skepticism deepened. I imagined my dad in his early twenties, with his polyester-dressed legs propped up on a coffee table, reading literature about the human condition—*Steppenwolf* and *Siddhartha* by Hermann Hesse and *Cannery Row* by John Steinbeck. When he married my mom, they moved into a converted corncrib in the middle of rural Michigan so he could help his grandmother with the family farm. My dad was still wrestling with faith. When my mom found out, she went into newlywed shock. To a theologically orthodox Christian like my mother, my dad's doubt seemed like the spiritual equivalent of an extramarital affair. The friction between them went on for weeks and months until finally my parents sat down and had a "come to Jesus" talk about keeping their spiritual lives separate—no praying together, no reading the Bible together—until my dad could sort through his search.

When I launched into my own skeptic phase as a teenager, my father ended up taking the brunt of my struggle. I started fighting with him, not over the usual curfews and chores—although we had those fights too—but over theology, metaphysics, and church. Our debates seemed robust and important, the kind of fighting every kid should have if she needs it. My dad and I would sit for hours on the living room couch and hash things out.

My mother reacted to these discussions with understandable fear that her kid was going to jump ship and leave behind the faith of her youth. Often, when Dad and I started debating, my mom walked out of the room, tired of listening to my drawn-out skepticism. But I was undeterred. I came home from the dentist one day and while standing in the kitchen, asked my dad, "Why did God make us with teeth that deteriorate, when half the world doesn't have the means to fix them? What does that say about God?" I had a whole litany of questions.

During this period, my dad started taking me out to breakfast. On Saturdays every few months, we would drive up to a hole-in-the-wall, no-name breakfast diner called Restaurant. It was the kind of spot cops go to after a long night shift or where fathers take their daughters while trying to stem the tide of incredulity. Dad and I sat in a booth and ordered orange juice and omelets. After conversation about school and work, we got down to the tough business of talking about God.

Some teenagers might have reacted to these conversations the way they might if their dad took them out for a safe-sex talk over pancakes. But I liked our discussions. I took notes. I still have some of them stuffed in my journals, as emblems of my systematic and almost obsessive pursuit of truth. I wrote in shorthand with one of the pharmaceutical promotion pens that my dad carried along with his hospital pager in his front pants pocket. Part of the breakfast ritual was asking to borrow Dad's pen, and then watching him rummage around in his pants pocket to find it.

"You ask good questions," my dad said once, passing

his pen across the table. "I don't always have the answers."

"I hate it when you say that. You're supposed to have the answers."

Some of the notes I took were written on my dad's medical pads. On a piece of paper headed with the motto, "Think of it first, Bumex, for diuresis you can count on," I scribbled notes from a breakfast conversation we had one Saturday about Fyodor Dostoevsky's *The Brothers Karamazov*. My dad and I were sitting at a booth in the middle of the restaurant. As we talked, the waitress came and set down heavy stoneware plates piled with food. Then Dad bowed his head and said a blessing while I looked sideways to see if anyone was watching. Public prayers still made me cringe.

"How can I be certain of anything?" I asked him after the prayer. "How can I be sure that what I believe is true?"

My dad paused between bites of omelet. "Well," he said, "in *The Brothers Karamazov*, the Grand Inquisitor criticizes Christ for choosing *not* to declare his divine power while in the desert being tempted by Satan. In so many words, he says to Jesus, 'If you'd turned stones into bread, if you'd shown your authority, the crowds would have followed.' By saying no to the temptation to show off, Christ left room for ambiguity about God, I think. He left space for mystery and uncertainty."

"Uncertainty seems like a cop-out. And anyway, why should the burden be on *me* to find God?"

"God rewards those who delight in seeking him. And God, like the Hound of Heaven, is also seeking you." The poem he referenced was a late nineteenth-century English piece he'd once read to us during family time.

"But doesn't religion seem like this system we use to make sense of things we can't make sense of? Doesn't religion diminish God?"

"Church and religion are *means* to God, not *ends.*"

"If Christ is the only way to salvation, the bridge to God, is it possible to cross the bridge without knowing it? Is it possible to know God without actually *becoming* a Christian?"

"Moses knew God," Dad said, reminding me of all the Old Testament Jewish prophets who lived before the time of Christ and still knew God in a very intimate way. "Think about C. S. Lewis's *The Last Battle* from the Chronicles of Narnia. The character of Emeth, fighting with Tash against Aslan and his army, had actually been serving Aslan without knowing it. His heart was in the right place. He aligned his devotion with good and not with evil."

"So what does that mean, then?"

"It's possible, I think, for someone to cross the bridge without knowing the name of the bridge. I think the lesson here is that we have to be open always to other people's knowledge of God, to their unique experience of God."

"Maybe so," I said, shrugging my shoulders.

I was listening in the way that teenagers do—with one ear turned toward my dad and one ear turned away. I had inherited my parents' faith and also my father's doubt. And yet, while I sensed my dad's companionship—I loved him for undertaking his own search and letting me take mine— I also felt alone in my pilgrimage. My father had made his choice to become a Christian and then a Quaker missionary. I still had my own road to take. Although in hindsight I see nothing oppressive about my childhood, at the time, I felt the kind of pressure that a pastor's kid feels. I was a missionary kid being raised to do good and to be good and to go make a difference. My parents were model Christians in the community. After a while, I started pushing back.

■ ■ ■

People who know my story sometimes ask me what I would have changed about my upbringing. They want to know what would have kept me inside the church when I wanted to step outside. (Subtext: What might they do to keep *their* kids inside the faith?) I tell them, "Nothing." I had everything. I grew up in a good church and in a good family. I had smart, well-educated Christians around me. They allowed me to push back. They let me doubt. They gave me room to ask my questions. But I wanted more space. In the way some teenagers feel the urge to sneak out at two in the morning and go smoke pot with their friends, I felt a growing urge to transgress boundaries in the realm of faith.

These subtle "transgressions" took place both in public and in private. They happened inside my head, in Sunday school, at youth group, and, most often, in discussion with my dad. One particular conversation with my father became a harbinger of the doubt to come. It marked a turning point in my pilgrimage. It cleared the path for my pending exit from church.

I was seventeen. My high school graduation was only a few months away. After going out for breakfast with my dad one Saturday morning, we drove to a Hi-Fi store to buy desktop computer speakers I needed for college. My dad went down one aisle. I went down another aisle until I came across a TV playing Eric Clapton unplugged in concert. I don't remember which song Clapton was playing as I stood watching, maybe "Running on Faith" or "Malted Milk." What caught my attention was not the song itself but its effect on the audience. I watched the people swaying. Clapping. Singing. They had the unmistakable demeanor of a congregation in worship.

I know what that attitude of worship means: I listen to music as prophecy. As memory. As longing. It feeds the hunger inside but also extends it. Most music is never good enough, hard enough, or heavy enough to fully satisfy, but when it does satisfy, you feel it deep in your gut. And if visceral impact is the mark of greatness, then Clapton was better than God. He was a man you could listen to and touch. A man wearing shoes and singing songs about grief and love and the San Francisco Bay.

Although it might seem strange to have a crisis of faith while surrounded by TV screens, that's exactly what happened. I discovered what philosophers call the problem of God's hiddenness: how am I supposed to relate to a God I can't see, touch, or hear? Why isn't God present the way Clapton is present? Why doesn't he have a grunge band and give concerts at the Key Arena so that anybody who wants to can buy a ticket?

Halfway through the second set, God would climb down into the mosh pit to dance with us, and the crowd would erupt with whooping at this revelation of divine booty-shaking proximity. Then while drinking a Corona at a post-concert bash with Pearl Jam, God would get up from his patio chair to say, "Can I take a turn on your Fender, Eddie? I haven't played in years." And that would be the moment we'd all been waiting for: God would play a deep, striking riff on the electric guitar.

"Dad, look at them," I said as my father walked up behind me in the store aisle. "Look at all those people."

"What about them?"

"Look at how they're listening. It's almost *religious*. All I see are people looking for a God they can't find."

My father nodded.

"How are we supposed to live with such ambiguity?"

"Well," my dad said, rocking back on his heels the way he always did while deep in thought. "You seek grace and truth and live as best you can in the conviction of what you know. It's all you can do."

"Why did *you* decide to believe?"

"I wrestled with this stuff for a long time. And then I knew I had to make a decision. I had to go one direction or another."

I turned back to the television screen. Staring at the Clapton concert just then, I felt the antithesis of what I'd experienced at my baptism years earlier. God was not a pastor standing in a river, holding me against the oncoming current. God was not a singer making sense of my longing. He was somewhere out there in the cosmos, other and untouchable or maybe even nonexistent, and I was left adrift, wanting the blessing of a priest but with no one to bless me except a man singing the blues.

PART TWO

BY-PATH MEADOW

In Pilgrim's journey, By-Path Meadow is the place that ends up leading him to the grounds of Doubting Castle.

Chapter 4

WAITING FOR GODOT

Whitworth University campus

I first met Damon Lucas in the courtyard of the English Department where I did my undergraduate studies. Dressed in a long black trench coat, he was holding a cigarette in his right hand and coughing. The skeletal branches of winter trees framed his figure. As I walked down the courtyard stairs on my way to class, he lifted his head from coughing and said to me as if we were already midconversation, "Have you ever heard Morgan Freeman's voice? I could listen to him read the yellow pages."

73

Damon was larger-than-life—dramatic, quick-witted, and demonstrative. On a college campus, you couldn't miss him. He dyed his hair pink or blue depending on the month. He wore frumpy sweaters and shuffled around in flat shoes looking like an old man crossed with a punk rocker. As the only child of a Presbyterian minister, he was by his own confession torn between orthodox religion and "orthodox" hedonism.

"I believe in Calvin's doctrine of total depravity," he said to me once.

"Why, because you like being depraved?"

"Yes, I like being depraved," he said. "But I'm trying to be good; I'm a Triple Whopper with cheese and vitamin supplements afterwards."

"You should be a Catholic, Damon."

"I don't believe in transubstantiation, but I like their communion better. The ritual gets you out of your world. I love that stuff."

"No, you should be a Catholic because you need confession."

"What I really need," he said facetiously, "is to figure out a way to reconcile hedonistic living with the teachings of Jesus."

Damon smoked and cussed like a heathen. He indulged his sexual appetite. But at heart he was still a pastor's son, knowledgeable of the doctrines of Christian faith and wracked with longing for a good old-fashioned gospel Jesus. One minute he was talking about growing up in San Francisco as a kid who adored the band Public Enemy, and the next minute he was expositing the book of James. I think

Damon and I were alike in more ways than we knew at the time. He was a pastor's kid the way I was a missionary kid, both of us trying to make sense of our religious upbringings. He found himself standing on the same threshold that I did and in that way came to play a role in my own search during college.

"I'm Damon," he said, crushing his cigarette, tossing the butt in the trash, and then holding out his hand.

"You're wearing Birkenstocks in the middle of winter," I said. "You're crazy!"

Underneath his black trench coat were white sandaled feet without socks.

"You're a new English major, aren't you?" he said.

"How can you tell?"

"I don't know, you look fresh and clean." He paused. "Hey, why don't you come downtown tonight with me and some friends? We'll be at the Mercury Café, nine-ish."

The Mercury was an old downtown coffee shop located in between bail bond shops, pawnshops, and the county jail. When I arrived that night, I found Damon sitting outside in a courtyard that opened to the winter sky. The trees overhead had been strung with long, draping lines of white lights. With hands stuck in my coat pockets in the shy, uneasy manner of someone on a date with new friends, I walked up to the table. Damon introduced me to a small group of his peers. I knew nothing about them, except that they were English majors who liked to wear black and read books. I knew even less about the content of their conversation. All evening long, they drank coffee, smoked, and stared at the stars while making obscure references.

"The guy who wrote the music to *Beetlejuice* is the guy who started the band Oingo Boingo," said Damon. "Did you know that?"

"And did *you* know," said the student sitting next to him, laughing dryly, "that *Beetlejuice* is what Joyce meant when he wrote 'the ineluctable modality of the invisible'?" (This, I learned later, was a reference to the James Joyce novel *Ulysses*.)

"Very funny," Damon said, and then looking up past the table canopy, "Is it still raining? They say April is the cruelest month." (And this was a reference to the poem "The Waste Land" by T. S. Eliot.)

I didn't say much. Sipping coffee and watching my breath form in the cold winter air, I was trying to figure out what in the world they were talking about and why it mattered. I felt the same cultural dissimilarity I had as a seven-year-old arriving in the US, having *E.T.* nightmares and wearing a missionary costume for Halloween. Damon and his friends had read books I'd never read and heard music I'd never heard. It was the late 1990s already, and I still didn't know the names of cultural icons from previous decades, like Andy Warhol or Tina Turner. Milli Vanilli might as well have been an air freshener. That night, college was more than just an undergraduate education. It became the cultural reeducation of a Quaker missionary kid.

■ ■ ■

As a senior in high school applying for college, I signed up to attend a small Presbyterian school called Whitworth Uni-

76

versity located in north Spokane only two miles from my parents' house. Whitworth offered me money. They made college affordable. They also offered a good Christian education without dogma—no faith statements to sign and no mandatory chapel attendance. Their marketing literature talked about the school's healthy tension between Christian commitment and intellectual curiosity, a tension that at the time resonated with my state of mind and made me feel safe the way Scott Edminster did. Whitworth seemed like the institutional equivalent to an old family friend playing Dire Straits and talking about doubt on a road trip to Montana.

After declaring as an elementary education major my freshman year—being an ed major and studying to teach children was what every eighteen-year-old Christian girl should do—I tried sociology my sophomore year. Sociology was the next best major for a Christian girl who envisioned herself saving the world through missions of social justice. But then right before my junior year, I switched directions entirely and declared myself an English major.

As an English student, I took a class in colonial literature and started looking at my missionary childhood through a more historical lens. I studied southern American literature and sat at a conference table discussing the religious themes of the Catholic writer Flannery O'Connor. I wrote a rookie paper comparing the nineteenth-century novel *Frankenstein* to the suicidal machinations of Kurt Cobain from the band Nirvana and a more mature paper on themes of evil and estrangement in the medieval work *Beowulf.*

But even though the literature I read shaped my view of history and human life, I was changed less by books and more by the people around me. The English Department became a haven for those of us who weren't quite sure where we fit inside the Christian tradition. The professors were Christian but not dogmatic. They were the kind of rabbi-like teachers you could go to and say, "I'm taking off my yarmulke; I'm not going to synagogue anymore," and they wouldn't blink twice or try to talk you out of it. They would listen and say, "Wait and see." In the end, they'd simply hand you a worn book off their shelf to read and ruminate on.

Some of the students in the English Department were the introspective, brooding-artist types who buried themselves in literature trying to make sense of life's perennial quandaries. The prelude to my drift and eventual departure from the church began in their company. They helped kickstart a cultural exploration. An awakening on the search. A new path on the spiritual pilgrimage.

Damon in particular became part of that new college community. A few weeks after we met, he invited me over to his house, a '70s rancher off campus that he shared with three other English majors. I had my first lesson in art and cultural literacy when I walked in the front door. Pinned up on the walls were posters from the films *Blue Velvet* by David Lynch, *Crimes and Misdemeanors* by Woody Allen, and *A Brief History of Time* by Errol Morris. The TV was tuned to Bill Moyers on PBS. In the living room, I saw ashtrays on every surface and in the kitchen, bottles of hard alcohol tucked in next to the paper towels.

After showing me the upstairs, Damon took me down to his living space in the basement, a large multipurpose room with an adjoining bedroom. On the fireplace mantel sat a copy of Shakespeare's *King Lear* and next to it a Homer Simpson bobblehead doll, a toy accordion, a Talking Heads CD, and a Catholic candle with a crucifix nailed above it on the wall — the Christ presiding over all things pop-sacred and kitsch. At least ten bookcases lined the walls, filled with CDs, DVDs, and what looked like hundreds of books.

Walking over to the shelf, Damon picked up a DVD.

"Have you read Robert Penn Warren?" he asked.

"I've read *All the King's Men.*"

"You know the voice of the demon in *The Exorcist?*"

"Oh jeez, Damon, you think I've watched *The Exorcist?*"

"Yea, okay," he said, waving his cigarette. Damon, I learned, had an encyclopedic memory for alternative and foreign film trivia that dated back to seventh grade, when his babysitter sneaked him in to see the R-rated *Barton Fink* at the local art theater. "It's Mercedes McCambridge. When I was in my *Exorcist* phase, I loved her deep cigarette voice."

He paused and held up the DVD for me to see. "She's the Sadie character in the Robert Penn Warren movie *All the King's Men*, directed by Robert Rossen."

"Good to know," I said.

Turning back to the shelf, Damon gathered up a handful of CDs, slung his backpack over his shoulder, and started up the stairs. We were on our way to a study session at a downtown bar called the Blue Spark. I had never been there before.

Located a few blocks from the train tracks, the bar had a small stage where local bands performed. Behind the stage were floor-to-ceiling windows that looked out at an intersection. All the night traffic became an unchoreographed background for the bands. Adjacent to the stage, bartenders stood behind a long bar, serving drinks to clientele on stools. The rest of the room was all booths and tables.

After we arrived, Damon and I took a back-corner booth and dropped our backpacks underneath the table. One of his roommates had planned to meet us at the bar after class and arrived a few minutes later. He slid into the booth next to Damon. I offered to buy us drinks.

"What do you want?" I asked.

Damon asked for a Whiskey Sour. His roommate asked for a Rum and Coke. I'd never heard of either drink. I was like a kid at a cocktail party—dazzled but out of place. I had no idea how to order a mixed drink. The last time I'd been in a real bar was for my girlfriend's twenty-first birthday, when some friends and I as a joke took her down to a back-alley dive called The Viking. But bars generally seemed foreign to me. As a kid, I associated them with rebellious, aberrant behavior in the same way that I associated non-Christian music with godless culture. They were the place where "bad boys" went. Now as a college student, that novelty became part of the attraction, part of my slow outbound passage.

Over the course of that night and subsequent nights spent hanging out at the Blue Spark, I learned how to start a tab. I ordered a cocktail without sounding ignorant. I sat on a bar stool and watched the incandescent lamps cast light onto the bottles of Bacardi and Jack Daniels and Crown Royal whisky.

"What can I get for you?" the bartender asked, turning to me. I was leaning against the bar, fiddling with my license

and feeling the cliché exhilaration of a Christian girl order-
ing hard alcohol for the first time.

"Two Rum and Cokes and a Whiskey Sour," I said.

While waiting for our drinks, I watched the band that
had been booked for that night. The four twentysomethings on stage were wailing on their guitars and howling
into microphones with the same kind of intensity you might
find in a street preacher wearing his last-days sandwich
board and pacing up and down in front of the corner post
office. Playing in a band, I thought, must be like getting a
cardiovascular workout for your angst. It seems cathartic.

"Have you ever read Samuel Beckett?" Damon asked as
I set down our drinks.

"No. Why?"

"Beckett's the Irish playwright who wrote *Waiting for
Godot.* He's brilliant. He's the cat's pajamas, the king of
despair, the voice of modern alienation. Everyone should
study Beckett, including you! I want to tear my teeth out,
his stuff is so good."

"What does he write about?"

"Beckett's all about men with regret and loss that they
can't get over."

"He didn't believe in God, did he?"

Damon's roommate, who was leaning back listening to
us, shook his head.

"It's tempting, isn't it, to throw it all out like that," I said.
"Faith takes too much work."

"But then we wouldn't be conflicted. English majors
love to be conflicted." Damon chuckled. "Anyway, I don't
think we'd be satisfied."

"Why do you say that?"

"We're plagued with longing the way Beckett is plagued with regret."

Damon described the plot of Beckett's *Waiting for Godot*—two hobos sitting around arguing, talking about nothing and trying to pass the time while waiting to be saved by some powerful savior named Godot who never comes. The title of the play, he said, was sometimes interpreted or misinterpreted as the subconscious iteration of a God-bating atheist who in his own cynical way might have been "Waiting for God." Beckett had never been clear what he meant by the title, really. Maybe he was an atheist the way Sartre was when he said, "That God does not exist, I cannot deny. That my whole being cries out for God, I cannot forget."

In the middle of our discussion, the band struck up a loud song and made it hard for us to talk. We opened our Norton anthologies and started studying until we couldn't study anymore. We drained our drinks, called for a round of water, and slumped down in our seats to listen to the band. I pulled out my camera at some point and took a picture. Damon and his roommate posed for me with their cigarettes dangling out of their mouths, looking like the pensive artists and writers that we all studied, admired, and aspired to become someday.

We took ourselves so seriously. Most people in the world don't have the luxury of sitting in bars having existential crises. Sunk in ennui, we were like the twenty-year-olds who sometimes loiter in urban parks, smoking and playing chess. You just want to say to them, "Get a job. Do something." But we were also sincere college students hashing out the search, sitting in the shadows of a bar talking about Samuel Beckett and hoping that his art—his life—might throw some sweeping searchlight over the dark path in front of us. We were lost, trying to make sense of our privileged, confused lives and looking diligently for something or someone that we didn't know how to name.

■ ■ ■

After hours of studying and talking, Damon and I gathered up our books and walked down the street to his car. He owned an Infiniti, a large luxury vehicle with a black leather interior that looked like a hand-me-down from someone's dead grandmother. Before we got in, Damon opened the trunk, showed me a six-cycle CD system mounted on the inside, and selected a handful of discs for us to listen to on our drive.

"You look like you're trying to sell me drugs," I said, "opening your car trunk in the dark like this."

Damon looked amused. "I'm the apostle of odd art. Leonard Cohen, have you heard him?"

I shook my head.

"This is one of the staples that I share with my disciples," he said, sliding the CD into the player.

Damon, I learned, derived a certain pleasure from bestowing his knowledge of art and pop culture on less knowledgeable peers, his disciples. He carried us into the inner circle like a godfather ushering someone into the mafia. Driving back home, Damon took me through a lesson in modern music history. He introduced me to Talking

Heads, Muddy Waters, and the Smiths. He listed their names in biblical genealogy and taught me who begat whom in the long lineage of artists. His pop culture was less mainstream and more indie-vintage, less Milli Vanilli and more Velvet Underground.

"This is 'Venus and Furs,' by Velvet Underground," he said pulling up to a light and taking a drag from his cigarette. He always smoked as he drove, flicking ashes into the ashtray below the radio dial.

After "Venus and Furs," he played me "In the Upper Room" by Mahalia Jackson and then a song called "Knockin' on Heaven's Door." I'd heard it covered before by Eric Clapton, but I'd never heard the original.

"Who is this?" I said.

"Bob Dylan. If Jesus reincarnated as a rock star, he would reincarnate as Dylan."

I laughed.

"Dylan will be assumed into heaven with Elijah."

That was how Damon talked, appropriating Judeo-Christian rhetoric to talk about his love affair with culture and talking about culture as a way of reckoning with faith. Dylan was the lost prophet of Christianity sent to save us through the dashboard speakers of an Infiniti. He spoke out of the darkness to say, "Let there be angst," and it was good.

The lyrics of the song had nothing to do with faith; it was a story about a dying cop. But that was the great thing about listening to music out on the road. You could revise meaning. You could make a song your own. As a twenty-one-year-old on a search, I felt that night the same brooding introspection I had in my late teens while listening to *The Secular Collection.* The music made my heart ache. It carried me out into the open-sky sanctuary of folk song and longing. It reminded me of sitting by a dying campfire as a child listening to my father play the harmonica in the dark.

I had grown up in the Christian church. But at that moment, caught in the dichotomy between sacred and secular, the best of so-called secular music held more promise. It had a searching, get-your-hands-dirty quality that felt right, a cuss-when-it-hurts quality that I didn't find at church. The Clapton concert that I'd seen years ago all of a sudden made more sense. Sitting there in Damon's car with city lights passing over the windshield, I found myself wondering again whether something as simple as music might offer more spiritual satisfaction than a hard-to-find God. Wondering whether the religious longing in my heart could actually be satisfied with something other than religion.

"That's good," I said after a while, turning to Damon. "He's good."

"He's the man," Damon said.

Chapter 5

LETTERS TO GOD

My senior year, I lived off campus in a house shared with three girlfriends. Two of my roommates were English students and the third was a theology student. We had books all over the house. Next to the toilet, poetry collections. On the dining room table, anthologies and commentaries. On the arm of the couch, novels and nonfiction. Both for class and on my own, I was reading books that reflected in title and content my growing sense of existential search. While my dad had read Hermann Hesse and John Steinbeck during his skeptic phase, I read *The Heart Is a Lonely Hunter* by Carson McCullers; *Another Country* by James Baldwin; and *Look Homeward, Angel* by Thomas Wolfe, a turn of the century, semi-autobiographical novel about a young man on a self-directed search for meaning.

Every day, I hauled around campus an army backpack stuffed with these books and others. After class in the afternoon, I would come home, sling my backpack onto the floor of my bedroom, and then spend hours typing English papers on an old behemoth computer that sat on my desk. The computer speakers were the same ones my father had bought for me at the Hi-Fi store where I watched the Clapton concert. Often while writing, I listened to music. Next to my desk I had a CD tower of music collected from over the years.

One evening after finishing a paper for my British literature class, I sat down on my bedroom floor for half an hour and started filing through the CDs. I found movie soundtracks and other miscellany. Most of the music, though, was Christian music that I'd grown up with as a kid. One disc at a time, I started pulling it all out. I picked up a Michael W. Smith album with songs titled "I Hope You Find Your Way," "Hand of Providence," and "True Devotion." I found an old Amy Grant album called *The Collection* with songs called "Father's Eyes," "Angels," and "Emmanuel."

I set aside probably a dozen different albums, as if I were going through my closet and getting rid of clothes that didn't fit anymore. When I was done separating the music, I put the Christian material in one discreet stack and everything else in another stack. I dropped the Christian

CDs into a paper bag, set the bag by the bedroom door, and then the next day, dropped it off at Goodwill.

The fish symbol on the back of my car met the same fate. Standing in my mother's kitchen one afternoon, I pulled the butter knife out of the silverware drawer, walked out to the curb, and started chipping the Ichthus sticker off the back bumper. I was purging myself not of faith necessarily, but of a particular *kind* of faith and of a Christian culture that I associated with spiritual certainty. I didn't want anything to do with it. I didn't want a Jesus fish on my car.

Although it took only a minute or two to break off the main part of the Ichthus decal, I spent another ten minutes trying to scrape down the faint outline underneath. The glue had left a light fish-shaped mark on the aluminum bumper. I did the best I could to remove it, but some of the residue remained. When I was finished, I picked up the pieces of silver plastic from off the pavement, walked back inside the house, and dropped them in the kitchen trash.

I made other changes in my life too, changes that echoed both the Ichthus removal and the CD dump. Becoming an English major had split my college timeline into two distinct eras—"BE" (before English) and "AE" (after English). Externally, the change manifested itself in fashion choices: BE, I wore long feminine skirts and flat-heeled shoes. I wore my hair shoulder length or longer. AE, I chopped my hair off. I wore short skirts and platform clogs, masculine Levis and button-up shirts. Internally, the change manifested itself in different habits: BE, all my friends were unambiguously Christian. I sang in the student-led praise band. I went to Bible study with my floormates and attended chapel. AE,

I had new friends that were more ambiguously Christian. I stopped singing in the student-led praise band. I stopped going to Bible study and attended chapel less frequently.

The changes in my lifestyle weren't as dramatic as they could have been. Some people in their early twenties go off the deep end and do drugs for a few years. That path in the end might be more efficient. Get it over with. Exercise your demons. Then exorcise them. My demons were hidden and harder to catch. In the same way that Ben and I as teenagers didn't stop listening to Christian music when we started listening to mainstream music, my internal conflict revealed itself during college too. At the same time that I was stripping an Ichthus from my car bumper, cutting my hair, and spending time in bars, I was still a college kid doing what Christian college students do. I went to classes taught by Christian professors. I roomed with Christian peers. I pulled toilet-paper pranks on guy friends who were training to be pastors. More important, I still went to church at Knox. I even taught Sunday school.

Every Sunday, often after a late night at the Blue Spark, I drove down to the church at the corner of Knox and Post and co-taught junior high Sunday school. The class met in McCleod Chapel, a small room off the sanctuary balcony with stained green carpet and an out-of-tune piano. I knew the room from growing up in the church. In the same room ten years earlier, the daughter of a church elder and I had skipped service one Sunday and spent the whole hour dropping pencils down through a hole in the wall. Off in the distance we could hear the voice of the pastor preaching from the pulpit.

The church had changed a lot in the interim. Not long before I started college, Van took a head pastorship at a Presbyterian church in western Washington and then lost his wife in a head-on collision. Joel retired from Knox to run for city mayor and soon after separated from his wife and moved out of the house. The falling apart of the head pastor's family somehow foreshadowed the falling apart of our church too. Over a period of years, pastors came and went. People left in droves. In the incipient stages of my drift from the church, my spiritual home seemed less like a shelter and more like a house with its roof half torn off from a storm.

In the midst of that turmoil, I was teaching junior high Sunday school. Some of the kids in the class were children of longtime churchgoers. Some were kids from the neighborhood who came from small scruffy houses and didn't know the Pentateuch from a comic book. In the same way that college interns every summer had been Jesus-loving superheroes for me, I wanted to be a role model for these kids. It seemed like the right thing to do, being present in their lives the way others had been present to my life as a kid.

Good intentions aside, though, I didn't exactly think through whether I was the right person to be teaching Christian theology. Somewhere during the spring semester, my own confusion started slipping into my Sunday school lessons. One morning, I trudged up the stairs into the classroom, set my Bible down on the table, and said, "Today we're going to discuss questions about faith." I launched into a lecture about how asking tough questions was part of faith and if God couldn't stand up to the muscled, fist-punching questions, then faith wasn't worth having in the first place. Even C. S. Lewis had said that. We had to be honest with ourselves and with God the way Job in the Old Testament had been honest.

Halfway through my introduction, I thought to myself, this lesson might be a little much for thirteen- and fourteen-year-olds who care more about schoolyard crushes than cosmic meaning. But I'd been their age once. Questions about God and the human condition had gotten mixed up in my pubescent struggle. Some of these kids probably had questions too.

"If you could ask God any question, any question at all, what would it be?" I asked, passing around paper and pens. Some of the kids played with the pens, holding them like cigarettes between their lips. Others bent over their desks writing. The co-teacher sat in the back row of the class, smiling. Back when I turned thirteen and started asking tough questions, he had been one of my Sunday school teachers.

"Take your time," I said. "Think about it. Then write it down on a piece of paper and sign it, like a letter."

After the kids finished writing, I asked them to fold their letters and pass them up to the front. After promising anonymity, I read the questions out loud one at a time.

Dear Lord, Why are some people so wicked when you made them special? Why do they want to lie to, hurt, kill, and steal from others? Amen. From Amy.

Dear God, Will you let my mom get the money from Shelly and Kendra so we can pay rent bills and have enough money left over so I can get a bike? Amen. Aaron.

Dear God, Why do my parents fight and hurt each other? I feel sad when they fight. I go and hide in the closet. Love, Joshua.

Dear God, Why don't you talk back to us when we pray? Sincerely, Max.

The questions lacked theological sophistication but in their simplicity seemed more incisive and difficult. They felt like evidence against belief. Reading them aloud that morning, I experienced the same frustrations I had while standing in the Hi-Fi store as a seventeen-year-old. Why isn't God more accessible? Why isn't God more like a real father who takes kids out to breakfast at the local diner?

After class had ended and the kids filed out, I walked across the hallway to the church balcony and, while over-looking the sanctuary, reread the questions to myself. They were just as sobering to read the second time as the first. When I was finished, I folded each letter in half. Then I shoved them all into my NIV Bible and closed it. They sat trapped in the middle of the Psalms. In so many words, I was saying to God, Here, you deal with it. This is your prob-lem. If you want my allegiance, make sense of this mess.

Chapter 6

AFRAID OF BEING THE BOLOGNA SANDWICH

Me in San Francisco

I was offered drugs for the first time at a so-called rave. An English major friend of mine and another student invited me to a dance club out in East Sprague, the red-light district in Spokane. We put on tight-fitting black clothes one night and carpooled to the club at ten o'clock, driving past the prostitutes and neon lights on Sprague to an old warehouse that had been refurbished for raving.

At the front end of the room, DJs stood on a stage mixing music under a spotlight. All the walls were painted black. Small disco balls hung from the ceiling with just enough dim light to illuminate a long, deep room. In a glance, the dancers on the floor looked like nocturnal bats might look while congregating under a bridge at night—huddled in groups, folding and unfolding their wings in the muddy darkness.

We kept to ourselves, mostly. One of my companions was a diehard fan of electronica who could name every sub-genre of music ever composed on a computer or a mixing table. He explained the nuances of so-called house music as we danced. After an hour, the three of us took a break and moved onto an upper balcony that looked down over the main floor. We talked and watched.

After a while, someone approached us and said very nonchalantly, "Hey, you guys want some E?" by which he meant Ecstasy. He offered it to us with none of the evil-eyed flair or trench coat sales pitch they warn you about in elementary school drug-awareness class. He might as well have been offering breath mints.

I remember thinking to myself, this is one of those moments when change could be quick and simple. One minute I'm hanging out at a warehouse rave; the next minute I'm experimenting with illegal, low-level amphetamines and eventually working my way up to the toxic stuff. But that wasn't my style. My kind of rebellion was more complicated and covert. I had a 4.0 GPA to defend and a Sunday school class to teach.

"No thanks," I said. Who needed Ecstasy? Being at a rave

club, like being in a bar or listening to Bob Dylan, put me close enough to what I saw as the sacred-secular line. More and more, though, I found myself closing in on that line. Riding it. Watching it, the way a highway driver watches the center line out of the corner of her eye and hums along its narrow edge trying to decide when to pass and when to pull back.

In our friendship, Damon and I rode that line together. He played the self-appointed chauffeur, driving the missionary kid out of the proverbial bush and down the road to the American Cineplex. He introduced me to James Joyce, Samuel Beckett, and the blues. But then I introduced him to Africa, Idi Amin, and the Quakers. He subverted his jealousy for my missionary childhood by teasing me. "While you were in the rice patties with Jesus," he would say, "Michael Jackson was doing the moon walk."

Everything we did betrayed a perceived tension between the church and the world. After an evening at the Blue Spark Bar and a music drive in his car, we would hang out in the basement of his house eating Cheetos and debating Scripture. We watched godless, despairing Ingmar Bergman films at the same time that we talked openly about God and faith.

"When you hit your knees," Damon said one night, "put in a word for me with the Big Guy, 'cause this train is bound for glory!" He added an expletive for emphasis.

"Damon," I said, chastising him. We were at a Shari's Restaurant sharing a brownie and studying.

"Sorry. I need to stop saying that. I might go to seminary."

"I'm not sure seminary is the place for you. You need

something to push against. Go to New York and study theater."

'"New York's the epicenter of godlessness."

"Then you can convert atheistic New Yorkers to agnosticism," I said facetiously.

"Can't we bend the rules, God? I got them this far. You know how hard it was to get them to just *wonder*?"

"That's good enough, why not," I said, both of us laughing. Then Damon looked at me and said, "By the way, I like your new hairdo. It's very chic."

For January term, I had taken an extension course on contemporary art in San Francisco. I studied films, murals, and modern art. In my off-school time, I found myself taking small but noticeable risks. I went dancing with friends at a gritty discotheque in the red-light district and watched a team of cops make an arrest ten feet away from me. I walked by myself around the city late at night. And I dyed my hair red. Everybody dyes their hair red when they hit an identity crisis. I might have been more original. I bought Clairol Spice #2 from Walgreens and then stood in the clawfoot bathtub at my hotel applying hair dye that turned my head the color of the Golden Gate Bridge.

When I came home from San Francisco with a shock of red hair, my mother gave me the kind of disapproving look that mothers give when their kids go off to California to dance at discotheques and dye their hair. She stood in the kitchen with her hands on her hips and said, half-joking, half-serious, "I didn't give birth to a daughter with red hair." I overheard her say to my father later, "Why are we spending so much money to watch our daughter lose her faith?"

My mother wasn't so much decrying my new hair color as she was noticing its symbolism.

A few months after dying it, I had my hair cut in a dramatic A-line that draped along my jaw.

"Thanks, Damon," I said, brushing the edge of my hair. "I like it too."

"You're the cat's pajamas, you know that?" he said.

"You said that about Beckett."

"It's the highest complement I can pay." Looking at me then with an expression of desire, he said, "Do you like me?"

"Of course I 'like' you, Damon."

"But do you like me in *that way?*" He scraped his fork across the plate. I looked away and then back at him.

"I'm sorry, Damon."

He paused, then launched into an allegory about love. Imagine I was in a magical forest, he said, and down from heaven came two platters. One held a rich three-layer cake and the other had a bologna sandwich. I (Andrea) might want the bologna sandwich (another man) because it's more practical. But it's also tasteless and boring. On the other hand I could choose the rich, unique chocolate cake (Damon). The cake is more fun to eat. Secretly, down deep, it might be the one I really want, even though the bologna sandwich seems like the more sensible choice.

Wincing at Damon's strange and not-so-veiled love proposal, I said, "What if in the end I don't *want* the chocolate cake?"

"But in principle you *like* the chocolate cake, right? So we should give it a shot. We have common interest in art, literature, and existential quandaries. Why can't we try?"

"Because I'm not interested."

"How about sixty years from now, if we're both widowed and living in an old folks' home? We'll hobble on our walkers and listen to Bob Dylan in the lounge."

"Maybe then, Damon," I said, feeling the ache of self-imposed loneliness. "Maybe when we're old and have things figured out."

■ ■ ■

Damon liked me, I think, for being a studious English major and a Sunday school teacher at the same time that I was dying my hair, going out to bars, and questioning faith while slumped in a leather booth seat. He liked me for my being conflicted. But that conflictedness was exactly what made me hard to catch too, not just for him but for others. I didn't want Damon the chocolate cake. But truthfully, I didn't want the bologna sandwiches either.

For my first official date as a college student, I was asked out by a friend of a friend who attended a Christian college on the East Coast. He had a few errands to run on his way out of town and started our casual date at a Macy's department store in downtown, where he tried on a suit in the men's department. "What do you think?" he said, turning to me. I stared at scarves and not at him while the suit fitter frisked him in front of a tall mirror. I hardly knew him.

After the suit fitting, we went out for pizza. After pizza, he said, without asking my opinion, "I'm not finished hanging out. Let's go walk to the park." So we went to the park. After the park, we went out for coffee. By then, four hours had gone by. I was annoyed. On the way home, as the sun set behind the hills of North Spokane, he said with a smirk, "I was praying this morning to God, and I said, 'Andrea's a nice Christian girl.' So I ordered this sunset for you."

It was a dumb joke that made me want to roll down the window and vomit. Although I conjectured a lot from one exchange, he seemed to epitomize what I disliked so vehemently about some Christian men—a schmaltzy, static, and altogether uninteresting faith experience. If Damon was my first chocolate cake, then this guy was my first bologna sandwich.

During the same year, a college friend of mine expressed interest in dating. He was three years older and had all the qualities that most women look for in a future mate—kindness, thoughtfulness, and dependability. We hung out on weekends with mutual friends and studied for tests together.

"Kyle's interested," I told my dad one evening. I was at my parents' house for dinner.

"Why aren't you interested in him?"

"Because he's a good Christian boy."

"What's wrong with good Christian boys?"

"I don't know. They're boring, I guess."

"Kyle" asked me out one night while we were walking the campus, coming in and out of the sidewalk lamplight and wringing our hands behind our backs. In the most gutless, circuitous way, I told him I wasn't interested.

"Can't we just give it a try?" he said.

"I don't think I'm capable of being loved."

"What do you mean?"

"I'm too sad and confused inside to be loved." Translated into the language of my self-absorption, what I was really trying to say was, "No one understands me. No one is good enough to understand me. And you're not the right companion for my search because I'm not attracted to you." I think we circled the campus five times before I made it clear that I was saying no.

The last man I rejected in college was an English major named Jeremiah, a Presbyterian pastor's son who read books by Edward Gorey and had big, brooding eyes. On the night that I met Damon and his friends at the Mercury Café, Jeremiah was there. He also played at the Blue Spark with his band. Pastors' kids, like missionary kids, had those hidden demons to exorcise. He sang on the stage of a downtown bar, crooning into a mic stand with his hair falling in his eyes in that very hip way that hair falls only for rock stars.

Not long before he asked me out, we had coffee together one afternoon at a café near the cathedral. We sat at a table next to a tall window looking out at maple trees and for more than an hour, talked about the topic of divine hiddenness. I remember the conversation clearly and how antagonistic I was in my tone, not toward Jeremiah but toward faith.

"If God wants all people to be reconciled to himself," I said, "then why doesn't he reveal himself uniformly, clearly? God is supposed to be the ultimate good. But not everyone in the world is given access to God, to faith, to goodness. For those who don't have access, in theory they're denied the ultimate good, at least in this lifetime, and if *they're* denied, why should anyone enjoy the privilege?" I was reiterating the refrain of an old gospel song: none of us are free if one of us is chained. In other words, none of us are found if one of us is lost.

"But don't you think God makes room for that deficit?" Jeremiah said.

"Maybe so. But still it seems unfair."

"Yes, it probably is. It's a tough question. Honestly, I don't have the answer."

I must have had an expression of distress on my face, because he looked concerned. "Do you still believe?"

"What do you mean?"

"Even with all your questions, do you still have faith?"

I paused, unsure of what faith even meant. Faith in Christ the Redeemer? Faith in God as the First Longing and the Last Haven? Faith as a story of future hope in the face of present darkness? Maybe in response to all of those possibilities, I said in a quiet, unsure voice, "I think I do."

Two weeks later, he and I took a long walk around an old city park in a scene that felt just like a Jane Austen novel. He was wearing a navy peacoat and pacing in a rose garden next to a woman whose hair was blowing in the cold fall wind. I could tell by the way his hands were clasped behind his back that he was trying to say something difficult. What he said exactly I can't remember. He spoke from the heart with the kind of invitation of love that gets either carried or crushed. Then after a deep breath I said to him, "Jeremiah, I think we're too much alike. I think we would drive each other nuts." Which was true. Both of us were brooders. Two brooders make for too much brooding.

But something more was going on too. I think deep down I feared that what Jeremiah liked about me was not me, per se, but the sum of my life: my stable family, my youth in Africa, and my good grades (a product mostly of socialization, I believed). In short, all the things I'd been given and none of the things I was at heart: unsure, confused, and trying to separate myself from Christian community.

Along with all the other men I turned down, Jeremiah became collateral damage on my warpath search to find what I was looking for. I was an outbound train. A car gathering speed on a downhill highway. Rilke's man rising from the table and readying himself to step over the threshold. Even then, I don't think I knew entirely what I wanted. The freedom to roam? A space of my own? Distance from childhood? I saw myself drifting from the church and everything affiliated with it, including good and decent men with good and decent intentions.

In the end, what I *should* have said to Jeremiah was this: "I am dissatisfied not with you but with everything."

Chapter 7

THE PRAYER
OF UNBELIEF

Me with John Sittser

During my senior year in college, I worked as a teacher's assistant for a Western civilization class called Core 250, a required course that surveyed all the major thinkers of Western philosophy from Plato to Freud. I had taken it as a sophomore and liked it so much that I signed up as a TA. At the end of the semester, the lead professor invited me and the other TAs to each give a brief "life application" lecture on what the course content meant to us. Every day that week, I spent hours putting together my talk as if it were the last word I would give before I got run over by a bus. I'm not sure why I cared about it so much. I felt almost pastoral toward all the students that I was TA-ing for, trying to shepherd them toward the search.

Standing at the lecture podium on the day of the presentation, I started my talk with a campy analogy about how studying philosophy was like dissecting bugs under a microscope.

"We've spent all semester poking Aristotle the Ant and Plato the Preying Mantis," I said, trying to be funny and failing at it. "At the end of the course, now, we need to step back from the microscope of dry, systematic analysis and think about the intellectual choices in front of us."

I leaned into the microphone. "After studying these philosophers, I can't stand up here and tell you what to do. But I can encourage you toward a process of seeking and asking questions in pursuit of truth. What does this mean? How do I live? Don't trade the turmoil for anything."

I felt the evangelical zeal of a tent preacher pausing before the climax of her call to Jesus, except that I was preaching a reverse conversion and inviting people not to come down to the stage but to leave the tent and go out into the world with their questions. The two key philosophical questions driving the Core 250 class—What *is* fundamentally real (metaphysics)? and How do we even *know* what's true (epistemology)?—were best answered, I thought, by avoiding easy answers.

"Whether or not you keep or lose your Christian faith, remember that it's more important to answer to your conscience," I said. "It's better to struggle as an active thinker than to become a passive Christian." In the middle of my lecture, the lead professor got up and walked over to the podium. "Thanks for sharing," he said tactfully. I had gone over the allotted five-minute slot and had to be ushered down off my soapbox so the last TA could come up and speak.

In retrospect, of course, I see the entire talk as a subconscious projection of a message I was really preaching to myself. *I* was the one ready to walk out of the tent and into the world with my fistful of questions:

What did Jesus have to do with literature and film and Friday night?

What did it mean that I was more moved and delivered by listening to music in my car than I ever was by a sermon from the pulpit?

Why had God made us with empirical senses that failed in any obvious way to detect and know him? What did it mean to go to church on Sunday and talk about invisible divinity, and then on Monday to go to school in a classroom where the professor entered the room in bodily form and dropped a book on the table with a sound you could actually hear?

As a teenager, I had carried these questions to my dad. After leaving home, I took them to professors and other adults in my life. I started going around with a spiral-bound notebook interviewing people about their spiritual stories like some overeager investigative journalist who thought she could cull the truth from a twenty-minute conversation. I went to my American literature professor from college, then to another English professor, then to a family friend — a smart, frank ER doctor like Scott Edminster. I wanted to know, *Why* is faith credible to you? What *reasons* do you have for your faith?

I met my American lit professor over coffee in the student union building at Whitworth and listened to him talk about the sense of clarity he felt in discovering the Christian faith. I met the other professor at a café midtown and listened to him talk about how art and music affirmed his longing for the divine. I met the ER doctor at her house out in the country. We went for a walk on a long winding road while she told me about her conversion to Catholicism and the personal meaning she found in faith, justice, and goodness.

The person I "interviewed" most frequently and thoroughly was a church history professor named Jerry Sittser. I had first met Jerry when I was seventeen years old, before even starting college. As a senior, bored with high school and feeling intellectually restless, I signed up for the Running Start program and took a few classes from Whitworth in my spare time. One of the courses was Jerry's Introduction to the Christian Faith, an overview of the central beliefs and practices of Christianity. I chose Jerry's class partly because, having grown up in the Presbyterian church community of Spokane, I knew he was a good professor and a good religious historian.

The real reason for my interest, though, had something

to do with Jerry's personal story. Two years after his fourth kid was born, a drunk driver slammed into the van he was driving, killing his wife, mother, and one of two daughters. He spent the next two hours waiting for the sirens while he paced the black edge of a highway with the body of his youngest son, still alive, slung over his shoulder. He, his two sons, and his eldest daughter survived the wreck.

In a very strange way that I cringe to admit, the accident, in my mind, gave Jerry spiritual credibility. If Jerry could survive that kind of trauma and still believe, I thought, then maybe faith was worth having. Maybe mine could survive. Listening to Jerry talk about faith was like listening to Nelson Mandela talk about forgiveness after being released from prison in South Africa. You had to listen. You had to take him seriously.

The story of the accident was almost myth to those of us who knew it. To Jerry, of course, it was a story of catastrophic pain and upheaval. His life tipped into chaos one night and then he spent years trying to climb out and put his family back together. As a single parent and a full-time professor, he spent all day grading papers, taking care of his kids, and tossing meals into the Crock-Pot. To help with the chaos, he hired a college student as a part-time nanny. When she graduated, he asked me if I would take over.

Jerry knew me as a student from the Introduction to Christianity course I had taken from him. He also knew me as the daughter of two prominent figures in the community. The assumption by extension, I think, was that, like my parents, I would be a dependable, stalwart Christian figure. "I take this very seriously," he said to me over coffee, after I said yes to his invitation to be the kids' caretaker. "You will be a model of Christian character to my children."

When I started, I was a nineteen-year-old single female playing a role I was hardly ready for. I went to David's junior high basketball games and sat in the bleachers next to moms who wore flower jumpers and talked about how their kids were going through "a weird mayonnaise phase" as if it were headline news. I attended Catherine's piano concerts. I played card tricks with Johnny even when he said to me with his lip pouted out, "You're not my mother."

Initially, the job seemed perfectly consonant with my identity. I was still my parents' daughter. I was a missionary taking care of three motherless kids. But after I entered my exploratory English-major phase, working as a nanny for a Christian professor roused the tension in my heart. It felt like teaching Sunday school on Sunday and then going out to bars on Friday to discuss godless Beckett plays. For his part, Jerry had no idea what he was getting into when he hired me. It was like picking up a rock that turned out to be a grenade with the pin half pulled. He didn't notice the transformation right away, but more and more, his nanny was no longer that stable Christian archetype.

I remember one afternoon in particular sitting at the kitchen table in the Sittsers' dining room, folding laundry and feeling out of place. As I picked up a pair of Jerry's briefs, I laughed to myself in a dark way and thought, I'm folding the underwear of a famous Christian scholar at the same time that I feel my own faith imploding.

Jerry, I knew, spoke nationally about faith and suffering. He counseled people who'd lost loved ones and opened mail from women all over the country who confessed their love to him after reading his book. Some of my friends, too, adored Jerry like a god. While lounging late at night in their dorm rooms, they tried to imitate his lecturing idiosyncrasies and joked with admiration about his frequent use of the phrase "redemptive trajectory." To *them*, I thought, folding Jerry's clothes, I'm touching holy relics. They should be nannying, not me. What am I doing here? Do I belong?

When Jerry came home from class that evening, he put down his lecture bag and then settled into the rocking chair in the living room. Behind him on the table sat my four neat stacks of laundry, one each for the kids and one for him.

"Sit down, pal," he said. He always called me pal. "Tell me about the day."

"Well," I said, "David called Johnny a 'butt' and then they got into a fight. That was the high point of the day, actually."

"How did it go?"

"I sent them to their rooms."

"Nice."

"Sometimes I feel like a soccer ref passing out yellow cards."

"You're the boss when I'm gone."

"Your kids don't lack passion, Jerry; they know how to make trouble."

"Well, they get it from their dad."

During high school, Jerry told me, he and some friends one night had "borrowed" pigs from a farm, stuffed them into gunny sacks, and almost released them in the cafeteria before someone told the principal and thwarted their prank. Then during undergrad at a conservative Christian school, he'd thrown a big party, broken the rules, and almost gotten kicked out by the college president before the dean interceded on his behalf.

"Are you serious?" I laughed. In the same way that I took comfort in my dad's skeptic phase, I was relieved somehow to know that Jerry had once gone through a wild phase.

"Don't tell the kids until they're older; they'll find out someday." He leaned forward in his rocking chair with an amused look. "Well, shall we start dinner?"

We walked into the kitchen and started prepping supper as we talked. Often after Jerry came home from work, he and I spent time going over schedules, discipline issues, or house cleaning. Sometimes our discussion had nothing to do with nannying at all. We talked about faith the way my dad and I used to over breakfast.

"Jerry, I have a question for you," I said.

"Yes? What is it, pal?"

"We say the power of God is in the church, but the church seems just as dysfunctional as every other human institution. It doesn't make sense."

"Well, the church is made up of fallible human beings. It's bound to be dysfunctional."

"Yes, but if the power of God has the power to redeem and transform, shouldn't we see *some* difference between the church and other human institutions? Shouldn't it stand out more in contrast?"

"Maybe it does," he said, moving around the kitchen. He always worked as he talked, the life rhythms of a single father.

"But what about the statistics on infidelity and abuse — they're not that different in the church community than any other community, are they?"

"The church does a lot more good than we think it does. Think about all the people working with refugees, the entrepreneurial efforts to found volunteer organizations, the Catholic hospitals, the universities. If you took all that out, society would be significantly worse. I'm not whitewashing the failures of the church. I'm just asking for a fair perspective."

"That sort of answers my question and sort of doesn't," I said, taking notes in my spiral-bound notebook as he talked. I was focused and fanatical with my questions.

"You're so intense, Jerry," I had said to him once in conversation.

"Well, that's the pot calling the kettle black, isn't it!" he replied.

As one of my interview subjects, Jerry was patient with my questions. He took them in good humor. He didn't judge me or tell me I wasn't Christian enough for his kids. He was a calm counterpart to my English-major peers, someone who had settled inside the house of faith and was speaking to me from within that space while I was standing in the doorway feeling ambivalent.

Every time he talked, and as he talked that evening in the kitchen, I listened to him the same way that I listened to everyone else — with simultaneous attentiveness and resistance. Nothing really satisfied me. Fundamentally, I didn't want to be satisfied. I was sure of being unsure, or at least I wanted answers only from the One who wouldn't give them. "I want to argue my case with God himself," said Job.

Before Jerry or I could expound more on my question, one of the kids walked into the kitchen and the conversation changed. I moved the laundry piles off the dining room table and set the plates around before we all sat down. When dinner was done and the plates had been piled in the sink, Jerry leaned back to the small shelf behind the dining room table and pulled off a Christian devotional book called *Streams in the Desert*. Out of his pocket, he took his reading glasses and set them on the bridge of his nose. Turning to the page bookmarked from the day before, he read aloud the way my father used to as part of family time.

Listening to Jerry's reverent voice and watching him turn pages with the careful deliberation of a man remitting wisdom to his young children, I felt pangs of nostalgia and confusion. Maybe the search couldn't be an end in itself. At some point, I had to commit to something. I had to pick a direction the way my father, in the midst of his own spiritual crisis, had to pick a direction. My dad and Jerry Sittser shared in common something I didn't—clarity of belief. A pathway. A sense of bearing.

After devotions, Jerry left for an evening meeting. I stayed to get the kids ready for bed. When Johnny's turn came, he pulled off his bookshelf the children's book *Are You My Mother?* and then crawled under the sheets. He liked to read aloud. After he finished reading the book to me, I slipped it back on the shelf and turned to him. "Let's pray," I said. We always prayed before I turned out the light.

Kneeling beside Johnny's bed, I remembered how my own mother had prayed with me every night as a kid. As part of the ritual, she sang an old Swedish hymn called "Children of the Heavenly Father":

Children of the heav'nly Father
Safely in His bosom gather;
Nestling bird nor star in Heaven
Such a refuge e'er was given.

After singing the lullaby, she would bow her head. Her prayer was a mother's supplication to God and her assurance to me that I would always have a refuge. As she prayed, it was as if my mother stood with me in the shadowed doorway of our house pointing into the distance and saying, "As you grow up, after you leave home, remember your final home. See it there, off on the far horizon? Don't lose sight of it."

The day before I left for college, I said to my mom, "I'll never be home again in just the same way, will I?" She looked at me with an expression of wistful relinquishment. I was moving two miles up the road. I might as well have been going to Mongolia.

As a way to stay connected after I left, she started sending mail—quotes from history, literature, and Scripture. She sent the letters out of love and out of a desire to see me rooted in the rich tradition of my childhood. One week, she sent me an excerpt from a letter written by the Southern writer Flannery O'Connor. It arrived in my mailbox as a carbon copy folded in three and stuffed into a business envelope. The attached sticky note said, "To Muff (my childhood nickname), from Mom." The letter had been composed by O'Connor in May of 1962 to a young man named Alfred Corn, who was corresponding with her.

"I think that this experience you are having of losing your faith, or as you think, of having lost it," she wrote, "is an experience that in the long run belongs to faith.... I don't know how the kind of faith required of a Christian living in the twentieth century can be at all if it is not grounded on this experience that you are having right now of unbelief. This may be the case always, not just in the twentieth century. Peter [sic] said, 'Lord, I believe. Help my unbelief.' It is the most natural and most human and most agonizing prayer in the gospels, and I think it is the foundation prayer of faith."

I read the quote, thought about it briefly, and then tossed the letter and the envelope onto a pile on my bedroom desk along with my "save for later" mail and old English papers. I didn't have the heart to weigh its meaning or be changed by it. But I didn't discard it either. For some reason I kept the quote, as if someday I might want to come back and read it.

Crouching down beside Johnny's bed that night, the prayer of unbelief was my only prayer. I felt insecure in my faith and insecure in my role as a nanny. I felt lonely too. No one prayed over me anymore. As a senior in college about to go out on my own, I was like the child still standing in the shadowed doorway, except that behind me, my mother had receded back into the house. In the other direction outside the house, I saw only desert and the faint line of a path.

In that dry place, I was supposed to say a prayer over Johnny. I was supposed to send him out on pilgrimage with a blessing. Struggling to find the right words and praying some bland, generic prayer about safety and good sleep, I thought, What am I doing? To whom am I praying? And why?

116

Chapter 8

A WASTELAND

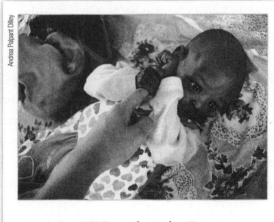

Andrea Palpant Dilley

An AIDS orphan in Kenya

When I graduated from college, my little brother bought me a T-shirt that read, "I have a Bachelor of Arts degree. Would you like fries with that?" I had no idea what I wanted to do after college. I had no idea if I could even get a job and no idea what kind of job would even suit me. While most of my friends were applying to graduate school or seminary, I felt directionless. Jerry helped me delay the need for immediate employment, at least, when he took a summer professorship at a university in Kenya and invited me to go with his family as the summer nanny. By then John, David, and Catherine were eleven, fifteen, and seventeen, respectively. After lining up a few part-time jobs for the fall, I packed my bags and left for Kenya with Jerry and the kids.

While sitting in the Spokane airport waiting for our flight, Jerry leaned forward with his head hung down in thought. "I miss Lynda," he said. It was a simple thing to say but maybe the most profound, when departure of one kind reminded him of a more significant departure.

After arriving in Nairobi, we moved into a small apartment on the Athi River campus and started into a two-month stint at Daystar University. Every day, Jerry went to class while the kids and I spent time reading books in the apartment, playing soccer outside, or volunteering alongside Kenyan college students who were building a new dormitory.

In the evening, Jerry came back from class often in the company of one or two of his students. Together, we would walk up onto the plateau behind campus and watch the giraffes gait through the wind-blown grass as the sun set over the plains. Standing on the plateau looking out at the savanna vista and the red horizon, I found myself returning to the homeland. I felt the kind of pride my father did when he took us once on furlough to southern France to see his French relatives' family homestead. "Look around," he said in so many words. "This is where I'm from. This is home."

"See that tree? That's an acacia," I said to the kids as we walked along the plateau. Or, "That flower over there;

that's a hibiscus. We had a hibiscus tree in our front yard in Lugulu." I taught the kids Swahili, the little that I remembered. I told David how as a kid I used to make soccer balls out of banana fiber. I showed John the vultures perched high in the trees. And I took Catherine with me to have our hair done up in a nearby duka shop. Sporting black extensions and sweating under the hot tin roof, I felt totally satisfied and content. I was back home again.

As a missionary kid pushing away from my Christian past, I was trying to *find* the past too. My subconscious needs contradicted each other. Deep down, I was still that "third culture" kid not content in her own birth country. Home, in both the pilgrim, spiritual sense and the earthly, geographical sense, was somewhere else. I thought that if I could just get back to the place I first remembered in the world, then I could find my way in the search. But trying to find the country of childhood was like watching stars in the night sky. By the time you saw them, the light traveling across that distance had already gone out.

For ten days that summer, I left the Sittsers and traveled with a Kenyan friend I'd stayed in close contact with over the years. On the first leg of our trip, we took a late bus from Nairobi. I couldn't sleep. I sat up watching trees go by in the night and then, after a while, I saw light at the horizon, darkness lifting, the long Rift Valley. We got off at Webuye and took a matatu taxi into Lugulu. It was the first time I had been back as an adult. We walked together around the hospital compound, an experience that turned out to be anticlimactic and disappointing for us both.

"My house has shrunk," Cathy said, looking at the cement

block house she had grown up in. My house, too, looked different. The sandbox was gone and the guava tree that we used to climb in had been cut down. Down the hill, the big forest Cathy and I remembered playing in turned out to be half a dozen scrawny eucalyptus trees lining a dirt path. Almost everyone we'd known, too, had moved back to Uganda or to other parts of Kenya. Lugulu seemed empty, like a house we lived in once that was no longer inhabited by the people we loved.

For me, what seemed even more disillusioning than visiting Lugulu was seeing the general decline of the country. When our family landed in Kenya in 1979, president Moi had recently taken office as head of a new republic that had broken off from British rule only sixteen years prior. Moi created what you might call a "mild" dictatorship. He established a single-party state, executed conspirators of a coup attempt, and set up police checks all over the country. I remember as a kid watching the uniformed policemen walk around with their guns as they searched the trunk of our car and demanded identification papers from my parents. Twenty years later, President Moi was still in power. His dictatorship had left a failing economy with miles and miles of slums rimming the southwest edge of Nairobi, not far from where I was staying with the Sittsers.

The missionary woman who lived next door to us on the Daystar University campus volunteered every week in those Kibera slums. Motivated by a desire to make good use of our time, the Sittser kids and I decided to volunteer with her. Once a week for the duration of the summer, we would pile into the back of her rickety van and drive ten miles into Nairobi.

From a distance, the slums gave the illusion of ocean—a sea of aluminum shanty roofs seamless and glimmering in the heat. But as you came closer and closer, what looked like sea from a distance turned into a landlock of poverty. Everywhere we looked, we saw squalor and chaos. Women were selling old vegetables. Men wandered aimless and unemployed. Children ran loose with wild dogs. On one of our visits, our van was caught in the crossfire of a rock-throwing riot as a government bulldozer went through plowing down illegal shanties. Something was always on the brink of falling apart or being torn apart.

Every Thursday, we drove down the narrow roads of the Kibera slums until we came to the Missionaries of Charity Mother Teresa orphanage. The campus had a wrought iron fence around the perimeter, several buildings, and a small dirt parking lot. The Sittser kids and I took direction from the Kenyan nuns and did what we could to take part in the daily work of the orphanage—in the preschool, the disabled ward, and the AIDS nursery. Most of the kids, we learned, were there because of severe disabilities. They'd been cast off into the hands of nuns. The rest of the kids, including the AIDS babies, were there simply because they were parentless.

Every time I walked into the AIDS nursery, I saw rows and rows of cribs filled with frail, preemie babies all bundled up in white blankets. Many of them were crying. Maybe the crying tripped some maternal alarm in me, I don't know, but I felt demoralized and almost debilitated. I kept thinking, What kind of planet do I live on? What kind of world is this, where babies get abandoned? Then I would see an African nun picking up one of those babies. She became Christ incarnate, the hope of peace and love. Only for a moment, though. There were so many babies to hold, she couldn't take care of them all at once. As a volunteer I helped every week, loving on them for a few brief hours. But what good was that? The babies kept coming. Most of them kept dying.

In the central building on the campus, the disabled kids slept in a space similar to the AIDS nursery, with the same long rows of metal cribs. Adjacent to that space was a large room where, during the day, nuns gave baths and served meals. The Sittser kids and I spent a lot of time there. We sat on mats singing songs with the orphans or feeding them porridge while the nuns cleaned pools of urine up off the cement floor. The whole experience for me was a reminder of how difficult and mundane it is to be charitable.

During one of our visits to the disabled ward, a little girl came running across the room crying and threw herself down in my lap. She pressed her head against my chest and with every convulsion smeared pus and blood from a wound on her temple. She cried and drooled and peed all over me. I was revolted by her and revolted by my own revulsion. I could barely hold her. She was a monster. So was I. I didn't have the heart to love her the way God, I thought, might love her. But then, where was he? Where was the almighty God in the midst of one girl's grief? I felt indignant, helpless, selfish.

Although I had a number of experiences like this at the orphanage, one in particular aggravated my questions about faith. Toward the end of the summer, the Sittsers and I along with our neighbor decided to take a group of the more able-bodied orphans on a field trip into the city. They all dressed up for the outing. Six kids in frilly skirts and button-up shirts climbed into a van and then waved goodbye to their caretaking nuns while we pulled through the front gate of the compound. It was the first time they had ever been outside the orphanage, much less the slums. We took them to the Nairobi public zoo and then out for lunch, and they were giddy all the way, singing together in Swahili at the back of the van as we lurched over the potholes in the road. It felt like taking street kids to the opera. Everything was amazing to them—the vinyl seats of the van, the paved streets, even the ketchup they had with their fish for lunch.

After listening to them sing for a while in the back of the van, I turned back to them, draped my arms over the middle seat, and then almost out of instinct started them on one of the Swahili songs from my childhood.

Mungu yu mwema (God is so good),
Mungu yu mwema (God is so good),
Mungu yu mwema (God is so good),
Yu mwema kwangu (He is so good to me).

I had grown up singing the song in church every week. As a family, we had sometimes sung it as a blessing before dinner, as a lullaby before bed, or as a road trip song, driving in our '67 Ford Escort through the Great Rift Valley. The orphans knew the song already and joined me.

Listening to myself sing in Swahili and remembering what the words mean in English, I thought, Of all songs,

123

why *this* one? Why am I singing a song about God's goodness while sitting in a van with six kids who were probably left at the front gates of the orphanage late at night by parents who couldn't afford to feed them? I felt my brain go black with outrage. Goodness didn't hold a candle to grief. And God did not seem good.

Earlier in the summer, our neighbor had told us a story about when her daughter was raped and trying to cope with anger at God. One of the nuns at the orphanage had said, "Tell your daughter to come and see the children, see their suffering, see their happiness. It will heal her." Sitting in the van that afternoon, I tried to feel the kids' blind, transcendent joy. But it was too hard. I felt glad for them and bitter at the same time. They were like little happy cherubs who thought nothing ill of the world even though the world had done great ill to them. They had porridge every morning. A crib to sleep in. A nun to get them dressed. They weren't hung up on the injustice in their lives, orphaned and motherless on the outskirts of a failing city, but I was.

After we came back from the orphanage visit, I sat on the edge of the bed in Jerry's bedroom while we folded the family laundry. Out the west-facing window, I could see the sun low on the horizon. The kids were playing in the field outside, kicking around a soccer ball with some of the Kenyan college students.

"Jerry, seeing all this suffering is really bothering me," I said.

"I know. It's sobering, isn't it?" He shook his head.

"You've thought about this more than anyone I know. How do you deal with the problem of evil? How do you

124

make sense of God's goodness, on the one hand, and, on the other hand, suffering?"

"In the face of great suffering, some people believe in God. I can't say that they're delusional. Nor can I say those who *don't* believe in God are delusional. We have been given the freedom to believe or not to believe, and we have to respect that. We choose. We live with the unanswered questions, with the senselessness of suffering and loneliness. There are *always* questions. What does it mean that children in an orphanage were abandoned, left to suffer alone? I don't know."

I stopped folding laundry and started writing in my "investigative" journal, scrambling to keep up with what he was saying.

"I watch those kids, Jerry, and I think about my own childhood. My father played me songs on his guitar. My mother read me books. I had this wholesome childhood that I didn't earn or deserve."

"Goodness is never deserved any more than suffering is."

"And I guess we have to think about the problem of good too," I said, almost begrudgingly.

"That was one of the first epiphanies I had after Lynda died. I was so angry. But after a long time I realized, if I say God *doesn't* exist because suffering exists, I also erase the source of the good. The reason I react so strongly to evil and to suffering is because I have a God-given sense of justice, rightness, and goodness. I can't have one without the other. It's a strange paradox. And besides, every worldview has to answer this question about suffering. We're all in this together. Saying that God doesn't exist doesn't make the

125

problem any easier. In fact, it might make it harder; it gives suffering less meaning."

"I can wrestle with suffering in theory, but in practice, when I'm holding a four-year-old orphan on my lap, what then?"

"Yes, it's very sobering," he said again. "We see suffering with no explanation. We ask the intellectual questions that have no answers, that must be lived, whatever that means."

Folding two socks together in his hands, Jerry said in the pragmatic tone of a scholar who is also a widower with a household to run, "Well, shall we get dinner going?" The sun had dropped below the horizon by then. The laundry was done, sitting in five neat stacks across the bed.

While standing over the stove cooking pasta for supper, I thought about my past growing up as a missionary kid and visiting sick patients at my dad's hospital for all those years. In high school, my family had gone back to Kenya for a summer and volunteered at a refugee camp. In early college, I'd worked at a church in Central Washington and spent every day with kids who came from troubled and sometimes destitute homes. Now at the end of college, I was volunteering at an orphanage in the slums of Nairobi.

Unlike Jerry, my own life at that point had gone untouched by loss, and maybe for that reason it wasn't my place to talk about it. But somehow it didn't matter. I'd seen suffering up close in other people's lives, suffering which I thought belonged in the public domain as evidence of a world that was profoundly messed up. It seemed personal to me. Like a lioness defending her young from attack, I felt an almost primal anger on behalf of other people's pain.

The poet Jane Kenyon said, "There are things in life that we must endure which are all but unendurable, and yet I feel that there is a great goodness." At the Mother Teresa orphanage in Nairobi, I witnessed that tension between suffering and goodness. I saw the theological paradox of Christian compassion: on the one hand, children who seemed forsaken by God, and, on the other hand, Catholic nuns acting out the call of God to bless the forsaken. But to me, that goodness wasn't enough. I felt a more pressing sense of confusion. The resurfacing of questions. The slow submersion of faith. I wasn't carrying around a handful of stones anymore; I was carrying a rock quarry of discontent. As I pictured the babies in the AIDS nursery, the whole world to me seemed like a wasteland of God's silence.

PART THREE

DOUBTING CASTLE

Doubting Castle is the home of Giant Despair and his wife Giantess Diffidence. On his journey, Pilgrim is captured by the Giant Despair and taken to his Doubting Castle.

Chapter 9

MY CAR,
MY CATHEDRAL

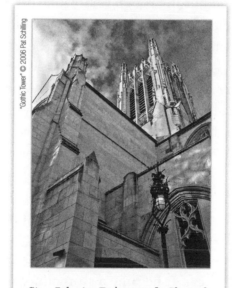

St. John's Episcopal Church

In the fall after flying back from Kenya, I packed up the boxes stored at my parents' house and moved into my first apartment in Spokane. I hadn't gone far from home. But maybe as an act of subtle individuation, I moved to the other side of town, twenty minutes away from my parents and from Whitworth. The place I moved into was a Spanish-style apartment with singular views looking both north and south. Outside my kitchen window rose the spires of one of the largest Gothic cathedrals west of the Mississippi, St. John's Episcopal Church, and out my living room window the city spread east and north into the foothills of the Rocky Mountains. I lived between the church and the world at a time in my life when I was pulling away from faith.

Putting together the rough semblance of an adult life, I started working four part-time jobs—freelance writing for a local paper, assisting a portrait photographer, nannying, and teaching Spanish at a private Christian school. I spent my day driving all over the city in a used blue Nissan that my parents had given to me as a graduation gift. (The old Plymouth hatchback, with its Ichthus ghost on the back bumper, had been given away to a grease monkey at Knox who planned to rebuild and resell it.) The back seat of my Nissan looked like hurricane fallout. Strewn everywhere were textbooks, school papers, and newspapers along with the occasional limp banana peel from a breakfast eaten on the run and tossed carelessly over the back seat.

I lived in my car. It became a symbol not just of my frenetic work life but also of my unhappiness. Often at the end of the day I would take a drive to clear my mind. After turning onto a long, two-lane highway somewhere outside the city, I imagined myself on the German autobahn hurtling forward through the night with no end in sight but the far horizon.

Often when I drove, I entertained the fantasy that, after climbing a long hill in the middle of nowhere, I might come to some final vista where the valley of the world would be laid out before me. All life began and ended there, and the mysteries of human existence revealed themselves with clarity and breadth. Once and for all, God would be unveiled at the horizon. The Truth would appear on the wings of rising hawks. Cathedral choirs would sing from a high cliff. That kind of clarity just didn't exist, of course. I might as well have harbored a fantasy about a comic book hero come to save the world from evil, terrorism, and teen angst.

While out driving, I always listened to music. I listened to German techno and angry indie rock bands. One night while sitting at a stoplight in the city with the volume turned up, I glanced over at the car next to mine and saw a young guy wearing a sleeveless tuxedo shirt and smoking a cigarette. I could hear his bass reverberating against the pavement. Somehow my bass must have been audible too, because he looked over at me with his head nodding to the rhythm of my music and smiled. He gave me an expression not of solicitation but of solidarity. Together, we were two people out on the road listening to music as part of the search for love and revelation.

In retrospect, I can see how lonely I was, feeling an existential connection with a total stranger. I don't miss that time in my life. Everything was in transition. In a short period I had graduated from college, spent a summer in Africa, and then come home and started into my solitary, post-college life. I found myself in between worlds the same way I had as a kid moving from Kenya to the US, but this time I was debilitated by the rupture of transition not from one country to another but from college to independence.

My community, especially, had changed. Some of my

college friends had married and moved away. Some, including Damon and his roommates, were busy finishing up their last year of school at Whitworth. We spent time together only once in a while. In their place, I had started hanging out with colleagues from the weekly arts and culture paper that I wrote for. They were the kind of artists and journalists who would get together at downtown wine bars or at art parties in urban loft apartments, the kind of hip, interesting people who could talk about everything from vintage skateboards to classic literature to the milieu of modern discontent. Most of them were nonreligious too.

One of them was named Luke. He was an art gallery owner who also happened to be my former high school English teacher. I sat in his classroom every day for a semester watching him pace back and forth in front of the chalkboard while pontificating on themes of American literature. I was eighteen. He was in his twenties. Years later, we reconnected through a mutual friend. We were peers with a weird history, and somehow that former teacher-student status became a deal breaker for anything romantic. It defined our friendship and made us free to be ourselves as two young and restless loners.

Luke lived on the South Hill not far from my apartment. We shopped at the same grocery stores and drove the same streets. Once, we pulled up next to each other in parallel lanes and while driving down the road at thirty-five miles an hour, rolled down our windows to say hi. "The ubiquitous Andrea Palpant!" Luke said. He was the kind of smart, likeable friend who used words like *ubiquitous* while the wind came whipping through his open car window. He was also the kind of friend I could turn to when my car got broken into one afternoon.

"Someone broke in while I was watching a movie at the Met Theater," I said to him while crawling out of my Nissan. On my way to the grocery store to buy cardboard and duct tape, I had passed by Luke's house and decided on the spur of the moment to ask for his help. He came walking out the front door. I watched him as he came, his tall, thin frame and his striking blond hair.

"In broad daylight?" he asked.

I nodded. "Whoever broke in kiped my CD player but left behind the CD. It was a disc of Rachmaninoff piano concertos."

"You mean he actually took out your disc before stealing the player?"

"Strange, isn't it."

"A thief with a conscience." He smiled.

"This is my third break-in, if you can believe that."

As we talked, Luke studied the window break and then went back inside the house and came out with a large piece of whiteboard. He held it up to the triangular hole and started cutting it to size before taping it down with duct tape.

When he was finished, Luke invited me into the kitchen and started searching through a stack of his CDs. We traded music every time we saw each other. The last time I'd been at his house, he and I had watched music videos together. One Saturday afternoon, we bought Chinese noodles in a to-go box and for hours sat in his living room eating with chopsticks and watching Brit-pop music videos from the early 1980s.

"Try this," Luke said. "They have a big stadium rock sound. You'll like it."

"Let's grab coffee sometime," I said, dropping the album into my purse on my way out the door.

After leaving Luke's, I spent half an hour in the back seat of my car, sweeping the broken glass off the seat and funneling it into a clear bottle that held shards from my last two break-ins. For some odd reason I displayed the bottle on my bookshelf as a souvenir of my car's theft history. When my parents called later that week to see how I was doing, I stood by the shelf, fingering the bottle and telling them what happened.

"You should get the window fixed soon," my father said, giving me the name of a repair shop down the hill.

"Who helped you patch it up?" my mother asked.

"A friend," I said, without giving a name. I could hear her on the line, breathing into the receiver and feeling edged out of her daughter's life. I remember very deliberately deciding not to tell her, knowing that she might disapprove of my spending time with a former high school teacher, even though nothing was going on. Not because it mattered. Because in some part of my heart I wanted to keep my past life separate from my present life, compartmentalizing things like a kid who keeps the mashed potatoes separated from the peas on her plate. I had friends that my parents didn't know and didn't *need* to know.

In the episodes of my pilgrimage, Luke was one of the traveling companions that I associate with the advent of my drift from church. He had no affiliation with my family or my childhood church community. I liked that about him and sought his friendship in part because of this "otherness." He also talked openly about his distrust of religion. As a lapsed Episcopalian who found his sacred space somewhere other than the church, Luke's faith story had been formed by one of the same questions that I asked myself almost every Sunday while slouched in a pew. If God exists, why is there so much suffering in the world? Why do babies get abandoned? Why do people go hungry?

For me, the question had something to do with growing up as a Quaker missionary kid and feeling a burden to ease the world's pain. For Luke, the question had something to do with his family history. His parents had died in a plane crash when he was a child. After college, he worked with street kids in Chicago, part of his past that resonated with the missionary kid in me. He was preparing to go into the Episcopal priesthood at the time. But then somewhere along the line he pulled out of seminary, never looked back, and left the faith, I gathered, because of the failure of the church and the failure of his childhood.

The loss kept coming too. His sister died unexpectedly in an accident. It was the third death in his family. A few weeks after the funeral and not long after my car break-in, I went to see Luke at his house.

"Here, follow me," he said, inviting me into his bedroom. On a drawing table up against a wall, he showed me a small photograph of his late sister lying next to a sketch of her face.

"My brother asked me to design a tattoo of our sister," Luke said, "as a kind of memorial. He wants to have it put on his arm."

I nodded.

"It'll never work." He picked up the sketch and turned it toward the light. "Faces never work for tattoos."

"Too much detail?"

"Yes."

"You shaved your hair off," I said, looking at his shorn blond head. He looked like an ascetic monk. Even this, the almost religious mourning rituals of a nonreligious man, meant something to me in my state of discontent with church. I don't know why, exactly, but I felt as if I'd been invited into the inner sanctum of his grief, standing there in his bedroom looking at his shaved head and the picture of his late sister. His lost faith felt consoling to me. Everything about him, even his sadness, seemed in a strange way like a refuge.

"I wanted an external symbol, like wearing black," he said, running his hand over his head and putting the picture of his sister back down onto the desk. "It's something to mark the time."

On our way to grab coffee that afternoon, we drove through a nearby neighborhood while listening to one of Luke's albums. Music drives had become one of the rituals of our friendship. We were like quiet tourists passing through the countries of other people's lives, watching a man mow his front lawn or a woman sit on her front stoop while her child played in a pool of light-rimmed water. Like an aimless soul out looking for a body to live in, I imagined what went on inside each house we passed. I thought to myself, Maybe if I had that life there, the one with the oak tree, the lawn, and the porch swing, then things would make sense. I could be happy.

Each drive had a melancholy, almost spiritual quality to it. The car was our cathedral. The music, our liturgy. The streets, our pilgrim road. That afternoon, Luke and I listened to the searching riffs of an electronica musician named Moby. As Luke drove, I leaned out the car window to let the wind lift my hair in the open air and felt the kind of peace you feel when you're with someone who understands the freight you carry.

"Save us, Moby!" I said. Luke laughed.

At the café, we sat by a window and talked in a pensive mood. Luke told me about his sister — the kind of person she was and what he missed about her. I listened, mostly. Luke had a laid-back, wistful disposition that made him easy to listen to.

"I don't believe there's a God," he said. "I don't want to know if there *is* a God," by which I assumed he didn't want to believe that a divine being could be responsible for all the loss in his life.

"It's hard to believe, isn't it," I said, remembering the slums of Nairobi. "Some days I'm disappointed in God, and other days I can't believe at all."

"There's too much suffering."

"I've never experienced the kind of loss you have, but sometimes I anticipate it, as if some great loss is going to happen to me. It just hasn't happened yet."

"No one escapes pain."

"Maybe all we can hope for are small good things," I said, referring to Raymond Carver's short story called "A Small, Good Thing." We had talked about the story at some point in the conversation.

139

"I saw two boys on scooters the other day. They wheeled up to a café drive-through and ordered lattes from their scooters. I think it's all I need to see. I can die now."

As he smiled to himself, I looked at him across the table with the longing of a lonely heart trying to find its home, one pilgrim pondering another. I liked him for his gentleness. For the honest questions he asked about God and life. For the books he read and the art he loved. To me, we were two companions out on the open road with our pilgrim burdens roped to the top of the car and our windows rolled down in the evening wind.

I wrote a lot in my journal during the time that I was hanging out with Luke. The entries were written in second person, directed anonymously toward my faithless friend and motivated by a deep subconscious need to make sense of the world not just for myself but for him too. I wanted to be comforted in my struggle; I wanted to comfort him in his. I wanted answers to my questions; I wanted answers to his.

Every time he talked about the cumulative loss of his late sister, mother, and father, my heart ached for him. The ache was deeper than empathy. I felt angry at God for abandoning my friend at the same time that I felt an intense longing for that same God — that deadbeat dad bumming around heaven — to come home finally and take care of us. Bless us. Be with us. Love us. But I couldn't do that for Luke. I couldn't will God to come home any more than I could will Luke's dead father back to life. I couldn't do it for myself either.

One night, I had a dream I was standing in Luke's kitchen. Luke went down into his basement and came up the stairs bearing in his arms stacks of oil paintings and pencil drawings—all the art he'd been working on for years.

"What are you doing?" I asked.

"This is my art."

"Why are you giving it to me?"

"I don't want it anymore."

He began, then, to hand me his art, piece by piece. With each handover, he asked me a question about faith. He sounded depressed and almost hopeless, as if his belief in goodness itself, not just in God, had collapsed. Giving me the very last piece of art, he looked me in the eye and with a sad, bitter voice, asked me a question I didn't know how to answer. "*Why* do you believe?"

Chapter 10

THE CHURCH WEARS HIGH-WAISTED PANTS

Knox Presbyterian Church

Wedged into the side of a steep hill between the cathedral above and the city below, the apartment building that I lived in dated back to the 1950s and, as far as I could tell, hadn't been renovated since then. The building attracted odd tenants, I think because it was so affordable. In the apartment kitty-corner to mine lived a woman, her two freckled boys, and her old barkless dog. The management prohibited pets. The first time I stopped by to say hi, the woman opened the door, stood there cradling a dog in her arms, and told me in a very paranoid tone of voice *not to tell*, as if she were concealing illegal Iranian weapons in her bathtub. Often after a long day of work, I would pull into the carport and find one of her little boys walking down the driveway with a duffel bag in his hand.

"Hi Jacob," I would say, climbing out of my car. "Where are you going?"

"Down to the park," he would whisper, pointing to the duffel bag.

Zipped inside the duffel bag, I knew, was their dog. Jacob was on his way to the park on a secret mission to let the dog take a dump in the grass. When the dog was done, he would stuff it back into the bag and walk home. He, his mother, and his brother were the secret-pet family in the apartment complex. I told his mom once that I wanted to have a cat. She advised me to put double stick tape on the windows, to prevent the cat from sitting in the windowsills and being seen. I never took her up on the idea.

Probably the most unusual tenant in the building was my upstairs neighbor, Will. He studied at the community college and worked at the hospital as a phlebotomist, a title I first confused with lobotomist. Neither one, phlebotomist or lobotomist, was the kind of vampiric neighbor I expected to have skulking around upstairs when I moved in. Will owned a pet snake named Voltaire, after the Enlightenment philosopher. Often in the evenings, he sat out on the back porch of our apartment building smoking cigarettes with Voltaire wrapped around his arm.

Will was a nice neighbor apart from his pot-smoking

habit and his loud music. At late hours of the evening, he listened to Pink Floyd through his high-end stereo system. All I could hear downstairs was bass and more bass, mammoth beasts beating on the ceiling.

At the time, I shared a one-bedroom apartment with a roommate. She slept in the bedroom; I slept in the living room on a foam mattress, which I folded up and stuffed behind a file cabinet each morning. Will's stereo system was located directly over the space where I slept. The first time I couldn't sleep, I went up and knocked, expecting some brute of a boy to answer the door. But Will was a midsize twentysomething who had blond hair that draped low across his forehead and eyes like those of a boy whose father never took him fishing. When I knocked, he came to the door and said without resistance, "I'm sorry. I'll turn it down."

We instituted an agreement then, a system for maintaining civility between us. I let him listen as late as I could tolerate it and he agreed to turn down the stereo when I asked. That was how our friendship started, two twentysomethings standing on opposite sides of a door wearing pajamas and deciding on terms of domestic engagement.

One Sunday night after a long, exhausting day, I could hear Will's music still reverberating from upstairs when I went to bed. After trying to sleep for twenty minutes, I went up and knocked on his door. No one answered. I went back downstairs and then half an hour later got out of bed again, went up, and knocked. Still no answer. It was midnight by then. My nerves had frayed. It was possible, I thought, that Will had left home without turning off his music or that he was sleeping drunk and couldn't hear my knocking.

The apartments had been built back in the day when men in white hats delivered milk to the back door. Inside each kitchen was an old milk door the size of a book. My secret-pet neighbor had once told me that a thief could break in through it just by lifting the inside latch with a slender object and then sliding his arm through the opening to grab the knob of the larger door. After rummaging in my kitchen, I took a butter knife, went back upstairs, and tried sliding it up and down the milk door to knock open the inside latch. After that, I tried a credit card. No luck.

Stepping back about to give up, I noticed the garbage door down by the floor. It looked large enough to fit a small body through the opening. I bent down and pushed on it and by some fluke chance, found it unlatched. At first, I was taken aback and stood staring through the gap into Will's kitchen. Going in didn't seem like the smartest idea. But I was alone and desperate for sleep, so I shimmied through, slipped onto the linoleum floor on the other side, and stood up.

Inside, the apartment was completely dark except for one lamp. I could hear the force of the music in the other room. As I stood there, I pictured Voltaire slithering out of his cage, trained to strike people who broke into the apartment. Feeling the boldness of a burglar, I moved slowly out of the unlit kitchen. Then into the dining room. Then into the living room. There on the couch lay Will, stoned, drunk, or God knows what. One arm was hanging limp off the edge of the couch.

"Will," I said. "Will ..."

He turned his head slowly, looked up with a blank face,

and then recognized me with a half grin, as if I were his beer muse come to tuck him into bed.

"What are you doing here?"

"I need to turn down your music, Will. I can't sleep."

Sliding my hand over the volume knob felt anticlimactic, almost, after breaking into his apartment. And yet, somehow, the whole experience seemed to typify my life at the time. I felt edgy, volatile, and unsettled. I found myself in tension with everything around me.

Every day, I was playing external roles that created friction with the state of my uncertain heart. For one, I felt unfit as the nanny for a Christian family. Jerry had prayed seriously before making the decision to hire me, having no foreknowledge at the time that I would start making my way toward the back of the church. I felt unfit for the private school where I taught too. Standing in the classroom watching my students pore over their Spanish dictionaries, I pictured their parents paying all that money to give their kids a Christian education. Feeling nothing like a role model for those kids either, I thought, Someone should vet me out and fire me.

The school enforced a strict dress code, so every morning before class I put on a skirt that draped below my knee. Every day after class, I swung my car into an alleyway and, while idling next to someone's garbage can, peeled off my skirt and slid on a pair of jeans for my next, less-formal job. I was convinced someone would discover that I was in fact not an adult but just a kid who was confused and playing dress up, slipping through the system as a full-time fraud working part-time jobs. I felt unprepared for independence, for the responsibility of waking up in time for work every morning, for having car insurance and remembering to buy vitamins. I felt even less prepared for making existential decisions about the religious beliefs I'd been raised with. Do I believe in God? Do I believe in Christ? Do I believe in the church?

I was still going to Knox at the time, out of habit more than anything else. Almost every Sunday, I backed my car out of the carport, bypassed the cathedral, and drove down the hill to the small brick church that had been a second home to me for the last fifteen years of my life. I knew the front door of that church the way I knew the front door of my parents' house. I knew the high mahogany beams and the stained-glass windows, the slight descent of the floor leading up to the pulpit, the choir loft, and the cross. More and more, though, I felt ill at ease in that space.

One Sunday morning when I walked into the sanctuary, I found my parents sitting halfway down the aisle on the outside. My mother had just finished playing the prelude on the piano and was settling into the pew. I took off my coat, sat down next to her, and perused the bulletin as the pastor stood up at the pulpit. "Good morning, and welcome," he said.

I looked around the sanctuary. At least a third of the pews sat empty. We had an interim pastor taking the role of the last pastor who'd left. In the midst of the instability, people were still leaving for other congregations. What remained of the church was hemorrhaging. For me, going to Knox felt like visiting a slowly dying relative in the hospital and seeing him hooked up to IVs and breathing tubes. The experience seemed painful, sad, and unpleasant. Maybe subconsciously I felt hurt and abandoned too—I don't know. Every Sunday, I watched the heart of my American childhood diminish down into a shadow of itself.

After the pastor had given the opening announcements that morning, the praise band filed up on stage to lead us in the time of singing. The lyrics to the worship music were always printed in the bulletin. The congregation stood and followed along with the lyrics. Opening the paper flap of the bulletin that morning, I saw the words to a song called "Shine Jesus Shine."

Shine Jesus shine,
Fill this land with the Father's glory.
Blaze Spirit blaze,
Set our hearts on fire.

As I leaned forward onto the pew in front of me, I couldn't bring myself to sing. I watched the praise band play, the drummer wailing on his drum set and the lead singer leaning into the microphone for the chorus, and thought, What does that even *mean?*

To my state of mind, praise music seemed irritating. At the time, the music was pulled straight out of the '80s— really peppy, clappy songs that made me feel like a bad Christian if I couldn't get hyped up about God. Some of the song lyrics sounded sentimental and vaguely sexual, talking about "Jesus, lover of my soul." Other song lyrics portrayed God as if he were the nice, muscular man next door who owned a calico cat, led rousing Bible studies in his living room, and answered the phone every time someone called. He held the receiver with a scrunched shoulder while stirring scrambled eggs on the stove and remitting divine advice. I mean, who could believe in a God like that?

The progression of worship, too, seemed awkward. After "Shine Jesus Shine," the pastor offered a quiet, reflective prayer and then the praise band started cranking out another up-tempo song. The transition felt jarring, as if someone were hitting my chest with a defibrillator in the back of a moving ambulance. I had the urge to crawl under the pew and read Catholic confessional liturgy or a Stephen King novel just to remind myself of something less optimistic and cheery. Chemistry mattered. The church had a good heart, but he listened to schmaltzy music, wore high-waisted pants, and drove his mama's Buick. I wanted the guy who listened to rock music in his light-blue Beetle with a couple of Russian novels sitting on the seat beside him. I wanted a church with less grin and more edge.

Once while visiting my grandparents' church in rural Pennsylvania, I had watched a middle-aged woman wearing light-pink stretch pants stand up for the special music part of the service and sing "The Star-Spangled Banner" with an exaggerated vibrato. American anthems should not be sung operatically in church by someone wearing stretch pants. Sitting in the front pew with my grandparents that morning, I thought cynically, This is the sort of thing that makes people want to become atheists.

"Christianese" came in all forms. Every time I drove out to my parents' house, I passed a small nondenominational church that had a reader board posted with catchy phrases like, "Want to know how to find the perfect will of God? Find out this Sunday!" The sign drove me crazy for its manufactured clarity. Of course, one bad reader board can't represent all Christian institutions. And of course, there was plenty of smart Christian art to go around, with cathedrals, concertos, and the Sistine Chapel. But at the tipping point of age twenty-three, I wasn't thinking about any of that. I was thinking about bad art—the reader boards, the praise songs, the stretch-pant operettas. Walker Percy's character Binx Bolling calls it the "Jesus Club." In a scene about the family going to mass in *The Moviegoer*, Binx says, "If they spoke to me of God, I would jump into the bayou," which is exactly how I felt about things. I'll dive into the bayou if you sing that song again.

My aesthetic frustration with church, though, wasn't nearly as potent as my ideological frustration. Cheesy songs were a mild infraction next to doctrines and ideas. After the praise band had finished singing "Shine Jesus Shine" that Sunday morning, the pastor got up and preached a sermon that I criticized for its entire duration. I scribbled questions on the bulletin and passed them down the row to my father. I wanted answers for everything. I wanted everyone to agree on the answers.

"Either the pastor's right or you're right, but you can't both be right," I told my mother after church, as if I knew exactly what was wrong with the world and with my parents and everything they'd taught me growing up. She stood there in the pew staring at me without saying anything. To her, I was sitting in a car in a driveway with the engine idling, ready to ram the ignition in reverse. Nothing could stop me. I might at any provocation back out suddenly.

In response, my mother leaned forward over the pew

and gave me a hug, as if to say, "I don't know what you're going through, but I love you anyway." She was right. She had no idea what my life looked like, what I did on weekends or who my friends were. She had no idea what I felt that morning after the service when I pushed through the doors at the back of the dim sanctuary and walked outside into the sunlight.

■ ■ ■

Even now with the advantage of distance and perspective, I can't entirely chart a clean progression of events leading up to my departure from the church. It happened over a period of about six months. Rather than being driven by conscious, "doorway of decision" questions—should I stay or should I go?—my departure seemed less decisive and more confused. I stood on the threshold of the church leaning out. Eventually, the critical mass of my weight forced me over the edge. That moment, that sudden, instinctive step, came unexpectedly while I was sitting in church one day.

When Ben's eldest daughter was baptized, I was invited to attend the service. On the day of the baptism, my parents picked me up from my apartment and we drove out into the open prairie country south of Spokane to a small Reformed Protestant church that Ben and his wife had been attending for a number of years. As we walked through the front doors, I could hear music off in the distance coming from a piano. We found my brother and his family in the foyer and walked into the sanctuary together. Wedged somewhere in the middle of the pew, I sat with my father on one side and my brother on the other. Ben gave me a hug that both comforted me and made me feel more lonely. He was all the things I wasn't—someone with his faith intact. Someone stable who had settled down and started having kids.

A few months before, Ben had stopped by my apartment with his two daughters one afternoon. He and I talked while the girls ate cheddar cheese that I'd pulled out of the fridge and sliced up for them. After they left, I found bits of cheese hidden all around the apartment for me to find, like little signs dropped along the trail by Hansel and Gretel. I found pieces on the windowsill. I found more in my potted plants and under my futon. Holding a handful of greasy cheese, I thought to myself, What if I left the church for good? How would I explain that to my brother's girls?

The baptism was sweet, water poured out on a child's head in a promise of newness and blessing. My niece walked up to the front of the church and stood in her Sunday dress with her hands folded politely in front of her as the pastor tipped a small stream of water out of a porcelain pitcher and said, "I baptize you in the name of the Father, the Son, and the Holy Spirit."

After the baptism, the pastor went up to the podium and preached a sermon that I will never forget. I remember it more clearly than I do the baptism that preceded it. I remember it because it marked the end of the life I had expected to live and the beginning of something else. The pastor began by reading part of Psalm 91.

If you say, "The Lord is my refuge,"
and you make the Most High your dwelling,

no harm will overtake you,
no disaster will come near your tent.

This passage, like many Scripture passages, is tough to interpret. If you read it as literal guidance, the psalm might say, "If you believe, *if* your faith is strong enough, *then* God will spare you from suffering." On the other hand if you read the passage as psalmist poetry, it might say something more subtle, like, "God is a refuge for those who believe." With the latter reading, the emphasis shifts back to the first two verses, which say,

Whoever dwells in the shelter of the Most High
will rest in the shadow of the Almighty.
I will say of the Lord, "He is my refuge and my fortress,
my God, in whom I trust."

The pastor at my niece's christening seemed to lean toward the more literal interpretation. I heard this message: those who have faith will be privy to God's full protection. They'll get a good insurance policy against pain. They'll have better coverage. Listening to the sermon, I thought, God doesn't promise to protect us from hardship any more than he kept Christ from it. The idea didn't make any sense. In fact, it seemed flat-out wrong. By that logic, people who suffered were people who lacked faith. And that just wasn't true.

For me, the issue of suffering still felt personal, even more so after coming back from my summer in Kenya. I saw everyone's pain. I wanted to ease everyone's pain. Even as a kid, I'd been that way. When my brothers dumped salt on a slug while camping once, I turned all Mother Teresa on them and started running back and forth from the campground faucet, dumping water on the slug trying to save it and screaming at my brothers for their cruel experiment on this helpless, spineless, slob of a creature. That was who I was back then, and it was still who I was sitting in church that Sunday. I wanted to save slugs and orphans from the cruelties of salt and lovelessness, respectively.

As the pastor continued, something inside me went up in flames all of a sudden. I leaned over to my father and blurted an expletive. Then I stood up in front of half the congregation, marched down to the end of the pew past my brother's family, and walked straight out of the sanctuary.

Pushing through the swinging doors at the back, I came into the empty foyer and sank down into a spare pew with my head in my hands. I was on the verge of tears. To be fair, it's possible that I stepped out of the sermon before all qualifications had been set forth. One pastor and one sermon were certainly not a fair sampling of Christian theology any more than a church reader board was a fair sampling of faith. But all the same, it meant something to me. The sermon provoked the deepest part of my heart and, by extension, my faith.

After a few minutes by myself, the sanctuary doors swung open and Ben came in and sat down beside me. "Hey," he said, putting his arm around me with a sigh. He didn't say much of anything. We just sat there in shared silence. I felt almost needy in my grief, leaning my head against my big brother and trying not to cry. I also felt understood. Without explanation, Ben knew why I'd walked out.

Some years before, we had visited some friends of my parents who were missionaries to Kenya from India. We were all together in the living room drinking tea when the topic of healing came up in conversation. During the discussion, the husband started sharing his views about how people just needed to pray and *believe* in order to be healed from illness. They needed faith, he said. That was all. While listening to him talk, Ben stood up suddenly from his seat and charged outside. My dad got up and followed him. "I feel like my rowboat is taking in enough water as it is," my brother said in reference to the spiritual doubt he was experiencing at the time. "I don't need something like this to rock my boat anymore. I've had enough."

I felt the same way that Sunday. My boat had taken in too much water. My discontent was overwhelming.

Leaving church on that particular day happened after I'd already drifted and my attendance had waned. I can't remember a specific date prior to that when I stopped going to church altogether. My decision wasn't conscious or dramatic. One day I just stopped going. In that sense, my niece's baptism didn't mark the first departure. But it marked a metaphorical departure, the critical moment when I realized I was stepping over the threshold of the church. I can't be here anymore, I thought. I need space.

Storming out of the sanctuary that morning, I felt the same volatility I had while listening to praise music at Knox and the same volatility I had while breaking into Will's apartment. I wanted the volume turned down. I wanted quiet and cessation. I wanted all the noise to go away.

PART FOUR

VANITY FAIR

In Pilgrim's journey, Vanity is a city through which the King's Highway passes. The yearlong Vanity Fair offers an enticing distraction for pilgrims on the journey.

Chapter 11

YOU DO NOT HAVE TO BE GOOD

When I was eight years old, my younger brother, Nate, and I one night had a sleepover at our house with Joel Edminster. At the time, Joel and I had an ongoing crush. We held hands at the skating rink and flirted in the back seat of the van while carpooling to church. When he came over to play on the day of our sleepover, he and I rode bikes together in the street for a while. Then we hopped off our bike seats and sat on the curb in close proximity, toying with the grass and talking until my mother called us in for dinner.

That evening, Nate, Joel, and I laid our sleeping bags next to each other in the basement and then went to sleep together. When I woke up the next morning and saw Joel's navy-blue underwear lying on the ground next to his sleeping bag (who knows why he took it off in the middle of the night), I was convinced in a fit of horror that he and I had somehow mysteriously had sex. We had after all "slept together" and his underwear was missing from his bottom, which gave me all the evidence I needed. I felt mortified for weeks until one day it occurred to me that conscious consent is usually part of the deal; it's hard to have sex when you're both deep in sleep and buried in separate sleeping bags.

What my first sexual "encounter" in the basement of our house had to do with my later sexuality might have been fodder for Freud. Sex was scary. Shrouded in mystery. It maintained this aura throughout my growing-up years, initially for reasons that had more to do with just being a kid rather than for reasons related to the stereotype of "Christian sex repression." My brothers and I and the Edminster kids weren't taught to repress sex so much as protect it. We'd all sat through classes at church designed to teach us that sex was "a special act" between two committed people inside the covenant of marriage. Sex was not for kids. It was not for messing around. (The word for "messing around," we learned, was *promiscuity*.)

A few years after the sleepover incident, I played Spin the Bottle one night with Joel, his sister Essie, and Nate. Our parents were inside the house having an evening Bible study. While they exegeted Romans in the living room, we hid behind a parked car in the driveway playing Spin the Bottle not with a bottle — we couldn't find one — but with a Granny Smith apple. Before we started playing, Joel said in a devious voice, "The Bible never said, 'Don't play Spin the Apple.'"

The apple was an awkward but symbolic substitute, the forbidden fruit bobbling around on the driveway. The stem served in place of the bottle mouth. For each of us, only one spin worked. Joel had to spin until the apple stopped at me — he wouldn't kiss his sister or his friend — and I had to spin until it stopped at him. The game was too rigged to really be a game. More than anything, we used it as an excuse for exploring our latent sexuality, pecking each other on the cheek while blushing and feeling the rush of transgression. We were way too conservative to kiss on the mouth or to try anything even *close* to sex. In the same way that God seemed like a strange, elusive secret our parents talked about while leafing through their Bibles, sex seemed like a strange, elusive secret.

When I was seventeen, my mom and dad sat me down at the kitchen table and in a very kind, parental spirit told me they wanted to buy me a purity ring. Evangelical Christians across the country were championing the abstinence movement, and every good Christian girl my age was wearing one as a symbol of chastity. My parents let me pick out the ring myself. I drove down to the jewelry store with one of my girlfriends and scoured through the glass cases until I found a gold band with a blue sapphire and two small diamonds. In the same way that I took for granted that I would always be a Christian, I took for granted the intended purpose of the ring at the time that it was given to me. Of course I would be chaste; it went without saying.

By the time I graduated college and moved out on my own as a young woman, not only was I a virgin but I was also painfully single. In the triplicate search for faith, love, and life purpose, the quest for love started emerging as the most dominant quest. I wanted a companion for the pilgrimage. While God seemed like that deadbeat dad who'd run off and left me, men seemed like a pretty good substitute. They were present. Embodied. Carnal.

First, I had to find one. As a twenty-three-year-old, I'd never been in a sustained relationship. My dating life seemed like a lab-rat experiment where I was injected with hormones and released into a maze with the implied directive to find a way through without losing my mind. I hit a lot of dead ends. Some of my friendships with men just petered out. For example, Luke and I drifted apart after a while. Nothing came of us.

Blind dates didn't work out either. Set up by a mutual friend, I went on a date one night with a local newspaper reporter in his late twenties. The day before, I had dinner with my friend Addison. Addison was from Philadelphia and said *horrible* with an *a*, as in, "That's *harrible*." She read voraciously and sang hymns by heart from her childhood growing up in a Presbyterian church. After getting to know each other, we took a road trip together to western Washington and on the way home sang "Be Thou My Vision" right after a long discussion about our struggle with faith. We shared the same paradox in our spiritual lives—feeling both resistance against and respect for the religious tradition we'd inherited. We shared, too, the same frustration with men.

"Give him a chance," she said, looking over the dinner menu.

"I know I won't like him."

"No you don't."

"Yes I do."

"Based on what?"

"Probability," I said. "I don't like most of the men I meet. They're dull."

Addison was insistent.

"It's a matter of mathematics, the number of people you expose yourself to. You have to try. Even now as we talk, we diminish our chance of finding love. Anyway, what I really mean by 'love' is that I'm hungry and need a hamburger," she said, turning back to the menu.

Two days later I took a chance and met the blind date at a café in downtown Spokane. Running late, I threw open the door of the café and saw a man sitting at a table against the wall. He was tall, maybe 6'2" and had a thick athletic build. I was not attracted to thick men. But what mattered were his eyes. I could tell in an instant that I wouldn't like him. From my judgmental view, I saw only his dull gaze and bland face and dismissed him immediately as someone who could never be my lawless, poetic chocolate cake. For forty-five minutes, I endured conversation about the state of partisan politics and contemporary journalism. I never saw him again.

Almost every dating story was the same. Something went wrong. The artist-painter who asked me out had wet, nervous hands and stared at me the whole time over coffee. Another man, confident enough to ask me out to coffee one Saturday morning while sitting at an adjacent café table, turned out to be a forty-year-old anesthesiologist with a teenage son. But age was not the real deterrent. I disliked The Anesthesiologist, as he came to be known in my dating history annuls, because he was an egoist who talked the entire date about himself and about a long motorcycle trip he'd taken through southern France. He offered to show me pictures next time we had coffee. But I declined.

I fared worse with Christian men. While sitting on the floor of a bookstore one day reading Spanish love poems by Pablo Neruda (which I used in my Spanish class as a teaching tool), I ran into a Christian teacher I knew. Standing over me in the bookstore with his tall frame, the teacher informed me that reading love poetry was in fact a kind of pornography for women. Lusty nudes for men, lusty words for women. I thought he was joking until he launched into a diatribe about how, in the sexual relationship between men and women, the woman was the cold, unlit house into which the man came to light his fire in the hearth. Feeling almost personally offended by his comment, I said to him in so many words, "Clearly, you've never met a real woman."

He was not the kind of man I wanted. The only men I wanted were men I couldn't have; that was the stripped-down truth. As a freelance writer for the local arts paper, I got assigned to a story about Ira Glass, the NPR host of *This American Life*. I was a big fan of his radio show. Before he came to town on his tour of the country, I interviewed him by phone one afternoon. He talked about breaking up with his ex-girlfriend. He talked about how making radio was a lot like making movies. And he talked about his first failed program—the sort of funny, self-effacing revelation that makes the girl on the other end of the line begin to like you.

At the performance, I met him down by the stage and introduced myself as the journalist he'd spoken with on the phone. I still have this wonderful photo that someone took of us standing there laughing—I can't remember what about—but it was the sort of passing flirtation that made me feel warmly human. After the show, I went out for drinks with a cadre of people from the local NPR affiliate. All evening, I watched Ira sitting across the table from me, leaning back in his chair, taking in more than talking, and listening the way a good storyteller listens as people go buzzing on about things.

I should have proposed when I had the chance, leaning over drinks in a small lounge to say, "How about it, you and me and American Public Radio?" The next day, he left. Now he's married and that's that. He was the sort of guy I liked to like, Ira Glass, confident, accomplished, and hard to have.

But these are just side stories. The real story is this. After college, I got involved with a man who was twice my age and, although I didn't know it at first, separated from his wife. Michael was a college professor from Oregon, the kind of man who drank gin and tonic and smoked cigars while listening to music after dusk. He was an old friend of a friend of mine. I met him at a restaurant in downtown Spokane when I went out for dinner one night with a college girlfriend. We walked into the restaurant, greeted my friend and the man sitting across from him, and then sat down at our table. When it came time to pay the bill, our waiter pointed to both men. "Those two gentlemen, over there." They had picked up our tab, he said.

The next day I stopped by my friend's house to drop off a thank-you note and ended up chatting in the kitchen with Michael. He was up visiting for a few days. At the end of the conversation, as I was walking out the door, he turned to me and said, "Would you like to grab lunch tomorrow?" I paused, looking at a man old enough to be my father, and then decided to take a risk.

"Sure," I said. "Why not?"

We had lunch the next day at a café in downtown Spokane. Over club sandwiches and Caesar salad, he asked me questions about my childhood—where I'd grown up and what books I liked to read. He loved music, so we talked about the music that he loved and the music that I loved. I felt seen and understood and flattered by his interest. I was attracted to him too. He seemed like something out of an old black-and-white movie from the '30s or '40s, the Cary Grant or Clark Gable type.

After lunch, Michael dropped me off at my apartment and promised to write. He flew back to Oregon the next day. A few weeks later, I got a package in the mail with a handwritten letter and a CD of a Brazilian musician. He thanked me for lunch and introduced the music he'd sent. The rest of the letter was comprised of short musings on the poetry project he was working on, the book he was reading, the balmy weather on the coast that day. The second letter he wrote came a week after the first. Prompted by a need for clarity, I wrote him back and asked point blank, "Are you married? Because if you are, I want nothing to do with you."

Michael wrote me almost immediately. He told me in so many words that he and his wife were in the middle of a divorce and that essentially he was a free man. Taking his character on faith as the friend of someone I respected, I wrote back and said, "Okay." Michael's kids were grown and out of the house, I knew, and he'd moved out too and lived alone as a midlife bachelor. I had a simple perspective at the time. By getting involved with a man separated from his wife, I saw myself as passing over not a solid yellow line on the road but rather a dotted yellow line. It looked legal but risky.

For months, Michael and I wrote letters back and forth. We didn't email and we didn't call. In the same way that seventeen-year-old girls fall in love with their high school art teachers, my initial interest in Michael was probably driven by a subconscious predilection for men in authority. He had life experience and history. In the same way that I liked Luke for his "otherness," I liked Michael for having no connection to my old communities. I took interest for other reasons too. I started growing fond of a man who wrote about poetry, music, and the small good things of life on the Pacific coast.

At the time that Michael and I started writing letters, I had long-standing plans to fly down to Palo Alto to visit a friend on my fall break. Only five days before my plane departed, I stood by the phone deciding whether to call and tell Michael I was coming. I knew from one of his letters that he had family outside the Bay Area and planned to spend his fall break there. I picked up the phone three times and then finally dialed his number. We had never spoken on the phone. The conversation was brief. Michael told me he would meet me at the City Lights Bookstore in the North Beach District.

In the last letter that Michael sent to me before we met in San Francisco, he wrote, "Today after work, I sat by the pool watching the sun set down behind the trees. The calla lilies are still in bloom, a whole white flock of them right next to my house. I've been reading Mary Oliver lately, have you read her? The poem about the geese?" Michael's letters had substance and intimacy to them, like small plates of nourishing food passed across the table from one traveler to another. He had enclosed Oliver's poem, titled "Wild Geese."

You do not have to be good.
You do not have to walk on your knees
for a hundred miles through the desert, repenting.
You only have to let the soft animal of your body
    love what it loves.
Tell me about despair, yours, and I will tell you mine.
Meanwhile the world goes on.
Meanwhile the sun and the clear pebbles of the rain
are moving across the landscapes,
over the prairies and the deep trees,
the mountains and the rivers.
Meanwhile the wild geese, high in the clean blue air,
are heading home again.
Whoever you are, no matter how lonely,
the world offers itself to your imagination,
calls to you like the wild geese, harsh and exciting—
over and over announcing your place
in the family of things.

I read the poem several times. I read it as the person I was then—a tightly wound child of the church whose only "deviation" had been playing Spin the Apple in my parents' driveway. I felt loveless and lonely and bound up in cerebral questions. Picturing the poet lying on her back in a field, I thought to myself, She isn't trying to get somewhere. She isn't fighting through a bramble thicket looking for the path. She's watching geese fly overhead in the evening sky. She's letting the animal of her body love what it loves.

Chapter 12

ATTICUS FINCH

Golden Gate Bridge, San Francisco

I flew in to San Francisco the day before Michael and I had agreed to meet and booked myself into the same hotel where I had dyed my hair red during college. After checking in, I threw my bag onto the bed, locked the room, and went out to walk the city.

All evening long, I wandered by myself and watched people go about their private lives: A store owner selling fish in Chinatown. A man in a business suit hoisting himself onto the trolley after a workday. A woman on a rooftop apartment, hanging her child's laundry to dry in the cold bay wind. I was alone, invisible from my past. No one who knew my name knew where I was at that time and place in the cosmos, what coat I was slipping on when the sun dropped below the horizon and the cold set in, which street I was crossing when the wind kicked up and blew my scarf behind me, or what I was thinking when I came up over a hill and saw the entire bay revealed, the dark blue antechamber to the great Pacific Ocean.

For the first time in my life, I went to a movie by myself. After walking through Chinatown, I bought a ticket at the movie theater at the Embarcadero Center. Behind me sat a middle-aged couple and a few seats to my left, a young couple. When the lights dimmed, I stuck my hands in the pockets of my coat and sank down into my seat. I knew hardly anything about the film. Halfway through it, feeling bored, I got up out of my seat, excused myself as I shuffled down the row, and walked out of the theater. By then, it was night out as I made my way back to the hotel.

The next day, I walked into the City Lights Bookstore and saw Michael. I felt the awkwardness of our meeting, two strangers who had planned to spend the day together. But we ended up having a good time. For eight hours, we walked the city, climbing the stairs to Coit Tower, exploring the muraled alleyways of the Mission District, and driving out to Ocean Beach in his pickup truck. We ate lunch at a café in the Haight-Ashbury District and drove past the townhouse on Lombard Street where scenes from Alfred Hitchcock's *Vertigo* were filmed.

At the end of the day, Michael and I went back to the North Beach District to have dinner at a small Italian restaurant. Sitting across from him, I felt a kind of contentment that I hadn't known in a long time. I was settled and at peace. The stones I'd been carrying, all those questions, dropped out of my heart almost unnoticed. My pilgrimage, too, seemed less urgent. If the search followed a dark, unlit road outside my door, then I was on hiatus at a high-end rest stop, drinking wine in the low glow of a room made for love and night jazz.

"I spent three weeks in San Francisco during college," I said fingering the neck of my wine glass during dinner. "Did you know that?"

"For what?"

"I signed up for an art survey course. While I was here, I dyed my hair red in a hotel bathroom. My mother hated it. I went dancing at a discotheque in the red-light district too, just a few blocks from here—down by the Condor Night Club and Big Al's. Not exactly star-A rebellion, but it was a start."

"The city has a wild side to it, doesn't it? Brings out the wild in us, I guess."

We talked about our respective childhoods for a while. "Why does childhood haunt us so much?" I said, thinking about my recent trip to Kenya.

"It's the unattainable past, the origin of ourselves that belongs and doesn't belong to us at the same time."

We stopped talking then and for a few minutes sat staring out the window at the passing trolley cars. After Michael paid for dinner, we left the restaurant and walked a few blocks to a small hotel where he had made reservations. He paid for two separate rooms, hauled my suitcase upstairs, and said good night to me as he closed the door behind him. I slept that night in a state of oblivion with a man I was starting to love two doors away. The next morning, Michael drove me south to Palo Alto and dropped me off at my friend's house for the rest of my stay. All weekend long, I thought about Michael. I wanted him, for asking nothing of me. For letting me be.

When I got home to Spokane, Michael and I started talking on the phone every few weeks. We kept writing too. He sent me novels by a Czech author named Bohumil Hrabal and books of poetry by Denise Levertov and Seamus Heaney. We read to each other over the phone and talked about the films we'd seen. Over a period of months, our friendship intensified from a distance until Michael flew up to Spokane for a guest lecture at a local university. I picked him up one evening at the park near his hotel. He was out for a walk, wearing a winter coat and coming in and out of the light of the street lamps with his hands in his pockets.

I drove us to a hillside pullout point that had a long vista overlooking the city and everything beyond. Staring off toward the mountains and speaking in soft tones, we talked and kissed all night long and into the early morning. Then we went out for breakfast at a greasy diner and ate pancakes and sausage as if there were no tomorrow. For the first time in my life, I saw myself less as a troubled heart and mind and more as a body just being an animal body. I wasn't helping anyone. I wasn't doing humanitarian good. I wasn't searching my soul for God. I was making out with a man all night and then eating pancakes on the white earthenware plates of a diner. He was the first man I kissed, a man twice my age who seemed kind and winsome. He was the chocolate cake worth taking, the impractical, decadent choice.

Michael went home to Oregon a few days later and we started talking on the phone every few days as if we belonged to each other, finally. We talked, as always, about books and film and poetry. We talked, too, about our age difference, and how he was having a midlife crisis and I was having a quarter-life crisis.

During all those conversations on the phone, though, we never talked about theology or religion. I didn't have the heart to revisit all the questions that had pushed me out the doors of the sanctuary. Although I knew he didn't go to church, Michael's formal worldview was a mystery to me. I gathered he was some kind of loose theist who preferred to read poetry about God rather than sit in a pew listening to a minister or a priest, but I never asked. He seemed unfettered by the big cosmic questions, and in that way his irreligiousness attracted me to him. He didn't take divinity so seriously.

For me, our entire relationship had everything to do with taking a break from "the search." While God seemed absent, Michael seemed present to me in the same way that Eric Clapton seemed present on stage, as an embodied man wearing shoes and singing songs about grief and love and the San Francisco Bay.

For months, Michael and I kept in touch until one night on the phone he said, "Marry me, Andrea." I paced on the wood floor between my living room and dining room, trying to find courage to say what I had to say.

"It won't last. What we're living now is just a dream; it's not real."

"We can make it real; we can make it work."

"I don't know."

"Take some time to think about it. I feel clarity; I know this is what I want."

"You're twice my age, Michael. We live in different worlds. You have children. I have brothers who would hang me out to dry for marrying someone twice my age," I said, half joking, half serious.

"We can't make this decision out of fear based on what other people think."

"I'm not making it out of fear; I'm making it out of practicality. We can't go on like this forever."

He paused.

"Are you sure?"

"I can't marry you, Michael. But I want to see you."

"Let's meet one more time, in Portland."

"For closure?"

"Yes, for closure."

After I hung up the phone, I took a glass of wine and sat on the back porch with the lights of the cathedral spire behind me and the city lights before me. After almost an hour, I threw my wine glass down against the cement and watched it shatter. I was crying, only vaguely aware that I had sunk myself into the kind of relationship your parents warn you about after it's too late. The kind of relationship that tries to fill the void of a wounded, tired heart. The kind of relationship before which you should pray the prayer, "Have mercy on me for all that happens in the wake of my need." The fact that Michael was technically still married and had a divorce to deal with never even came up in our conversation.

Although only in retrospect can I see how naive and undiscerning I was, I can also see that I gained — my search gained — from knowing Michael. He was a friend and a companion who helped me realize that I could be loved as the person I was, even with all my questions and confusion. He came alongside me at an important juncture in my pilgrimage. If leaving church was marked by stepping over a threshold, then Michael was the one holding my hand as I descended the stairs. At the base of the stairs, I let go of his hand and went on alone.

■ ■ ■

Addison came over to my apartment a few days after Michael and I talked. In a spontaneous act of low-level deviance, we drove to a downtown grocery store and bought a pack of smokes. I had my first cigarette that night while sitting on a park bench staring out over the Big Spokane River valley. Addison walked me through the steps, teaching the missionary girl how to draw nicotine into her lily-white lungs. In all those years of spending time with friends who smoked, I'd never tried it myself. After a while, I got the hang of it. We talked late into the night as the moon drifted high overhead and cast white light on the river down below.

"You know who I decided to marry today?" Addison said quietly. She knew about Michael. "Atticus Finch, from *To Kill a Mockingbird*. Don't you want to marry Atticus Finch?" She took a pull from the cigarette and handed it to me.

"Yes, I suppose so. He's handsome in that older sort of way, and kind."

"Life should be like one of those choose-your-own adventure books where the reader gets to decide what happens. You can have anything you want. You can marry Atticus Finch at the end of the story and live happily ever after. Why isn't it like that?"

"I don't know."

"Love makes me crazy. Someday I'll be playing Ping-Pong in a psych ward." Addison laughed.

"But at least with love, you have someone to watch over your craziness," I said in a wistful voice, coughing and handing the cigarette back to her.

A few weeks later, I drove down to Portland by myself, six hours south and then west along the Columbia River. Before I left, my mother called to invite me over for dinner with my brother and his family.

"I'm out of town this weekend," I said. My mother asked me where I was going.

"Portland," I said. She asked whom I was going to visit.

"A friend," I said, dropping the subject.

I picked Michael up from the airport. We spent the day holding hands and bumming around the city—stopping into art galleries, browsing through bookstores, and walking through the light rain. All day long, I felt as if I were sitting on the front porch of a house that was no longer my home, packed bags placed at the bottom of the stairs and the car idling in the driveway.

After dinner, we checked into a hotel in downtown Portland. Michael paid for one room rather than two. That night, I kept the law but not the spirit of the ring on my right hand, with two diamonds and a bright blue sapphire.

I had worn it all those years without really thinking about it. When the fire alarm went off at one in the morning, I gathered blankets around my body and waited outside the hotel with a crowd of evacuees, feeling exposed in more than one way as I stood under a street lamp next to a man with blue eyes and gray hair. After the alarm was fixed, we walked up the stairs to our room and went back to bed. I lay there in the dark next to a man twice my age. A man who was technically married, a man with no apparent religious convictions.

Feeling the start of a departure from everything that had come before and the slow subversion of my entire Christian upbringing, I thought, I should feel guilty, but I feel human.

Chapter 13

GANDHI LIVES NEXT DOOR

I met the actor Aidan Quinn once. I have a picture of me standing next to him with his arm draped around my shoulder in front of a tall spruce tree. I was visiting a movie set with him, James Spader from *Boston Legal*, and a few other actors when the makeup director said to me, "You should come over and say hi to Aidan; he's very nice."

Aidan Quinn was in *Legends of the Fall* and *The Mission*. He was also in *Bennie and Joon*, a movie produced in my hometown and shot mostly down by the Big Spokane River in a small shack of a house that Damon was living in while finishing up his senior year at Whitworth. "This is where they shot *Bennie and Joon*," Damon would say while giving tours of the house with a cigarette dangling from his mouth. At least I had something to make small talk of if I had to.

But small talk is easier said than done. Some people have the kind of quick wit that enables them to say the right thing at the right time. I'm not one of those people. Some people have the self-confidence to be calm around famous people. I'm also not one of those people. In the ten steps I took from the craft services table to the place where Aidan sat, all semblance of self-composure dissolved into flakes of ash. Lounging back in a chair holding a script, he looked up at me as I approached. Instead of saying something normal like, "It's nice to meet you," I went blank and said the most inane thing right out of the blue.

Gesturing toward the plain, brick wall of the house behind us, I said, "Interesting architecture, isn't it?" In any other context, it might have been a great pickup line. But not in this context. Aidan glanced over his shoulder and then looked back at me with a strange expression. The conversation never really recovered. One of the behind-the-scenes photographers came around with a still camera and insisted that he take a picture of us. Aidan got up from his chair and stood next to me for a photo that made us look either like an unhappy married couple or, more accurately, like a fan-weary actor and some awkward girl.

After that experience, I vowed never again to talk with celebrities on set. By then, I had quit my four-job rotation and taken my first full-time position at a film production company. Like most people my age trying to figure out what to do as an adult, I harbored conflicting fantasies about my future. I pictured myself as a crazy-sexy rock star wearing red leather and leaning into a microphone in front of a stadium full of fans at the same time that I pictured myself as the next Mother Teresa, wearing a linen sari and saving Calcutta's homeless from the dirty gutters. What I never pictured myself doing was working in film production.

After a history professor at Whitworth found out I was interested in media, he put me in touch with a company that eventually hired me as a writer and production assistant. I had no idea what I was getting into. Even after the cultural education of my college years, I was still at heart the missionary girl who'd grown up in East Africa. For me, taking a job in the entertainment industry was like a Mennonite farm kid from rural Pennsylvania getting hired as a disc jockey in downtown Philadelphia. I felt out of place.

On my first day, someone gave me the task of restocking the company fridge with soda that was meant for consumption by company employees and visiting Hollywood big shots. After I'd finished with the fridge, someone else summoned me over the loudspeaker to an editing suite. I found one of the company photographer-directors sitting in a swivel chair with his feet propped up on a table and his hands folded behind his head in a posture of confidence.

"I need you to go buy me four pairs of Levis and a couple of gerbils," he said.

"Sure, and a six-pack of beer while I'm at it." I thought he was joking.

"I need this stuff for an ad for a health-food store. They're sort of visual metaphors for health."

What I wanted to say was, "You've got to be kidding me." Instead, I said, "Okay, I'm on it."

I drove to the pet store and bought a couple of rats, because gerbils, according to the storeowner, were lazy nocturnal creatures and wouldn't do well for a fitness advertisement. Then I drove the rats back to work and stuck them in a cage in my cubicle where the two of them proceeded to defecate and procreate in rhythmic turns until the day of the shoot. I remember swearing under my breath and thinking, Where am I, and why do I have rats pooping and having sex on my desk? Thinking back to that moment and the months and years that came after feels almost surreal to me. I saw the strangest things and did the strangest things.

I once visited the set of a film called *Mozart and the Whale* and got to watch a teen-heartthrob actor who was listed as "#30 on the Hollywood Hot List" in *People* magazine one year crash his car into a stop sign on Third Avenue. I went out for dinner with some Hollywood executives from another film and listened to one of them do Darth Vader impersonations into his water glass while inadvertently name-dropping. "George is weird," he said, by which he meant George Lucas. As a production assistant on a credit-card commercial, I made small talk with a muscle man who turned to me in his white tank top and asked, "Do you think it hides my taper?" I watched buildings explode, drove a stunt car around the block for a B-rated movie, and stuffed myself into the back of a vintage Corvette as the backseat driver for a man dressed up in a pelican suit.

In the character vernacular of John Bunyan, I had joined an industry epitomized less by Pilgrim and more by Mr. Worldly Wiseman and the denizens of Vanity Fair. I found myself miles away from my childhood and suspended over the strange vaudeville stage of American entertainment. Part of me felt like a misfit. But part of me, too, felt pleasantly sedated by the shallowness around me. I was tired of questions, tired of urban slums and lost love. I didn't want to look back. I didn't want to search my soul. I didn't want to think about anything important.

Work gave me that space. Post-college, my work colleagues emerged in place of my English-major friends. They
became my new community, similar in camaraderie but even
one step farther removed—they weren't Christian kids pushing back against the status quo. Most of them didn't practice religion at all. Most of them didn't read philosophy or
study social justice. They were earthy, fun-loving people more
interested in the taste of a good microbrew or the light on a
well-shot film scene.

One of them was named Ty. He was a photographer at
the company and part of a group of twentysomethings who
hung out together at bars and film theaters. I had met him
for the first time in the editing suite when he asked me to
buy gerbils and jeans for the health-food store ad. He was
eight years older than me, had a tall, slim, athletic build,
and wore a soul patch on his chin that he trimmed like
a hip little facial topiary. I pegged him first as the nonin-
tellectual jock type. He talked about downhill skiing, jogging with his black lab, Annie, and collecting vintage Land
Rovers that he fiddled with and fixed up in his garage. He
seemed nice enough but not my type.

I took no particular interest in him until a family friend
named Henry told me that he had been the physician to
someone from our company who lost his wife to leukemia.
Henry and his wife, Karlene, had been residents in my dad's
internal medicine residency program. I knew and trusted
him.

"They'd been married a matter of days when she was
diagnosed," Henry said. He and I were sitting in deck chairs
at a backyard barbeque, holding paper plates on our laps.

"Just one of those tragic things. She was so young. I can't remember his name, I think it was Tay or Ty or something like that."

"Ty? Young guy, red hair?" I said.

"Yes, that's him," he said.

As Henry talked, my impression of Ty turned itself upside down. I had dismissed him first as being too "regular," like bland, lukewarm coffee, and then took sudden interest in the idea of some high-octane, espresso-shot sufferer who might hold the key to the human condition. Finding out his history was like finding out that Gandhi lived next door; it changed my view of things. The next time I saw Ty in person, I saw someone totally different. I saw a twenty-nine-year-old whose wife had been diagnosed with leukemia on their honeymoon, a man who nine months later laid her in the grave. We were sitting adjacent to each other in the company basement right before a big client party. The band was outside warming up. People were coming and going with chairs and sound speakers while we sat and made small talk.

"I heard you know Henry and Karlene," Ty said.

"Karlene's a friend of mine."

"She's a little old to be your friend, isn't she?" He looked at me with curiosity.

"I don't pick friends by age. I grew up around adults. I think I'm more at ease with adults than I am with my peers." I smiled.

"How do you know them?"

"Both of them went through my dad's residency program."

Ty nodded, then paused. "Henry was Janine's doctor," he said. "He took her case after she was diagnosed."

Ty told me about some of the complexities of her medical case and what the doctors had done in trying to save her. Although I can't explain why, exactly, his divulgence made me feel a deep spiritual longing for him. To me, experiencing suffering was like seeing the dark side of the moon. People who suffered had come near to some great mystery. The rest of us had to shimmy up close in order to vicariously experience that mystery, in the same way that people want to talk to astronauts who've returned from space. What did you see? How dark was it? How long did the darkness last?

"Let's go for a run sometime," Ty said. Somewhere between leukemia diagnostics and old friends, we had talked about running.

One week later we went for a jog, and after that, we started spending time together. We talked in the hallways at work and ate our lunch together in the company kitchen. We went to movies with mutual friends. When Ty had free tickets to a rap concert at the Met Theater, he called me. We sat in the balcony, watching rapper LL Cool J wipe down his perspiring back with towels and then toss them into the front row at teenagers screaming for a sweaty rap-star relic.

We hung out in bars too. When Ty went out with his friends one night, he called and invited me to come. I drove down, ordered a beer, and sat in a booth shooting the breeze with a bunch of tough-muscled production guys who crowed at my jokes in a brotherly way and made me feel beautiful.

"I like you," Ty said nonchalantly, smiling when his buddies laughed at something I'd said. A man likes it when you humor his friends.

When Ty's Land Rover was at the mechanic's shop one day, I gave him a ride home after work. We talked and listened to music together. After I dropped him off in the driveway of his house, he leaned through the open window in his casual, confident way and asked me if I wanted to help him organize a yard sale to sell his late wife's things. Somehow, in a state of irrational attraction, I agreed. What woman in her right mind not only falls for a man only *after* finding out that he's a widower but also agrees to help him sell his wife's belongings?

On a Saturday morning, I arrived at Ty's house just after sunrise and helped him price the shirts she wore and the bike she rode and the books she'd read only a year ago. He gave me a roll of burgundy upholstery fabric she bought before she died, which I used eventually to cover one of my dining room chairs. "Here, have this," he said handing it to me across a folding table piled with books and other items.

After the yard sale, Ty invited me to stay for dinner. While he stood over the kitchen stove sautéing vegetables, I walked around the living room looking at pictures of Ty's late wife while listening to his stories about her chutzpa and how she'd turned him down twice before agreeing to a date. I had asked about her.

"How did you meet?" I said.

"A mutual friend set us up."

"And then?"

"I called and asked her if she wanted to go out for coffee," he said. "She said, 'I don't drink coffee.' 'How about a beer, then?' I said, and she said, 'I don't drink beer.'" He laughed. "She was tough."

I laughed too, in an anxious way. The man I was interested in was standing in his kitchen talking about another woman.

After dinner, we went for a run together. I worked hard to keep pace as Ty ran up and down the hills of Rocky Mountain country with his dog, Annie, behind us. Back at the house, I slipped off my tennis shoes in the dining room, went to use his bathroom, and on my way out noticed something I hadn't seen before. On the wall hung a cross-stitch piece with the love chapter from 1 Corinthians:

Love is patient, love is kind.
It does not envy, it does not boast ...
It always protects, always trusts,
always hopes, always perseveres.

"Janine made that," Ty said, finding me in the hallway. "She had a good heart. Used to take care of a lot of kids as a physical therapist. She was good with kids."

He said it with a quiet, wistful voice, as if all goodness had died when his good wife died, leaving him a dry heart and an empty nostalgia for all things religious and virtuous. I stood staring at the cross-stitch piece wondering why Ty had left it in the hallway of his house, a reminder of the woman he once loved and a reminder of a God who seemed loveless in permitting loss and death.

At work, I'd heard stories from other people about how Ty took care of his wife in the hospital for months on end—

coming every day after work, talking with doctors, raising money to help pay massive medical bills. He watched her body change like a field in fall, diminishing in the wind. And when she died, he stood alone at the back of her funeral unable to speak and recoiled in grief. I was moved by all this, by the mystery of him and the history of his solitary heart.

I wanted him, too, for his lost faith. From conversations, I gathered that Janine had been a Christian and Ty a lapsed Christian when they started dating. He rejoined the faith when they got together and abandoned it again when she died. To me, he was a priest ordained by pain — someone to bless and be with me. Someone to understand my fractured faith. Together, I thought, we'd be sojourners looking for home.

I had other, less-intense reasons for my interest, of course. Ty listened to NPR and had a great vocabulary. One afternoon while we were standing in the work studio talking, he used the word *anomalous* in a sentence about river canoeing. English majors have an almost involuntary attraction to people who can command the English language; it's the ultimate seduction. All in all, he seemed like a good blend of chocolate cake — a smart, worldly artist with a wounded heart — and bologna sandwich — a man closer to my age and therefore more practical.

Ty and I started dating not long after we met. After dinner one night, we went for a walk through his neighborhood. He lived in an area of town inhabited both by bohemian artists and low-income families. We passed broken fences and kids scurrying around in the streets waiting to be called home by a mother who was smoking cigarettes on her sunken front porch. As we walked, we made small talk that burned down block by block into palpable silence and sexual tension.

By the time we walked up the steps of his house, we shared an unspoken understanding. I liked him. He liked me. He slid in the movie *A Clockwork Orange* and we sat back on the couch together with our bodies pressed side by side, two pent up, lonely people finding solace in slight contact. It seemed a little strange and maybe even uncomfortable to be sitting next to a widower while watching a drama that told the story of a wife's death.

After the movie was over, the lights still off, Ty shifted himself on the couch and turned to kiss me.

"I need to take this slow," he said. "This isn't easy for me."

"I need to take it slow too." I thought about all the letters from Michael that I had burned one day in my bathroom sink, dropping a lit match into the pile of paper and watching it turn to ash so that nothing was left behind for anyone to find and scrutinize. By then, he was on my mind less and less.

"I like you," Ty said.

"You mean I'm not a loser?" I said with the self-deprecating smile of a woman who's never really dated a man her own age and isn't quite secure in herself. I lacked self-confidence the way I had while making small talk with Aidan Quinn next to a brick wall. All of a sudden, I became the awkward missionary kid in the arms of a cool urban photographer.

"Take off your boots," he said, kissing me again. I was

wearing vintage-style leather boots that looked like the impenetrable armor of two small armadillos. I looked Ty in the eye without saying anything and left my boots on. We kissed for a while and then I said, "I need to go home."

"Stay the night with me. I have an extra bed in the guest room," he said, guessing at my hesitance.

"I had a good time. I'll see you at work tomorrow."

I pictured his bed up in the attic bedroom, myself rumpled up in the sheets where another woman used to sleep. I half wanted to stay. Spoon into him with the comfort of my body. Be the woman who saved herself by saving him. But I wedged myself out of the couch and walked across the hardwood floors of his house in my heavy boots.

The next day I called Ty to tell him I'd left my sunglasses on his couch the night before. I brushed past him at work, feeling attraction and confusion as he slid sunglasses into my hand on his way down the cubicle rat maze.

"He's complicated," a work friend said to me, stopping me in the hall after surmising my secret.

"What do you mean?"

"I mean he's complicated."

"But I like complicated men."

"You'll find out soon enough," he said with a tone of warning as he walked back down the hall.

Anyone with common sense who has read the handbook on human romance will tell you to avoid falling for someone who has suffered way more than the average human being. They are not the key to spiritual or emotional salvation nor are they a key to the human condition. My friend had read the handbook. I had not. After three days of "dating," Ty came over to my apartment, sat down on the futon, and said, "I'm not ready for this. I'm sorry."

"Okay," I said quietly.

"Let's just take a step back, get to know each other."

"Fair enough."

"I like you. I'm just not ready to get back in the game yet."

I didn't say much of anything after that, sitting on the futon with my feet curled underneath me. Turning my gaze away toward the mountains, I was one pilgrim letting go of another. I fought to maintain the dignity that collapses when a man tells you he's stepping off the train platform, leaving you there alone with your luggage and your fragile heart, pulling at its seams.

PART FIVE

THE SLOUGH OF DESPOND

The Slough of Despond is a miry swamp, one of the hazards of the journey. Pilgrim falls into the Slough and sinks under the weight of his burdens.

Chapter 14

THREE
FLAT TIRES

At the height of my crisis, I developed a propensity for getting into car trouble. The car embodied my anxiety. I broke the speed limit often and racked up enough tickets to jack up my insurance rates. I drove impulsively too. On my way to work one morning, I ripped off the driver-side mirror while pulling out of the carport. On my way home one night, feeling distressed and miserable about something, I took the steep turn up to my carport without slowing down and felt my front axle slamming down onto a cement barrier. My judgment error cost more than a thousand dollars.

Even with the vehicles at work, I got into trouble. It wasn't always my fault; sometimes things just went wrong. When two agency clients flew in from Portland for an editing session one afternoon, a producer sent me to pick them up from the airport. The agency, incidentally, was representing the car service company, Triple A. While driving sixty-five miles an hour down the freeway, I felt the front of the van start trembling and then the left front tire went flat. I veered onto the shoulder. After standing on the side of the freeway for a few minutes, wondering what to do, I hiked up my skirt and eased down into the drainage ditch to a cyclone fence. On the other side of the fence was a neighborhood and presumably a phone. I had forgotten my cell phone at the office. I have no idea why, but it never occurred to me to change the tire myself.

I took off my shoes first and threw them over — a sort of collateral to ensure my own follow-through over the fence — and then started climbing. The fence stood twelve feet high with no lateral support. As I clawed my way up, the fence starting bending toward me and shaking under my weight. At the top of the fence were cut wire spines. I threw my first leg over safely. But then as I threw my second leg over, my leggings snagged on the high spines and left me hanging by my half-ripped nylons. My skirt was still hiked up around my waist. I remember thinking, What in the world am I doing and how did I get up here? To freeway drivers going by, I must have looked like a self-hung scarecrow.

After a few seconds of surreal awareness, I threw my

weight down and backward, tore myself off the wires, and then crash-landed on the other side. I found a house with someone home and used his telephone to call the receptionist at work. A production assistant was sent to the airport to get the agency clients. A production grip was sent to get me. He came peeling around the corner in his red Corvette to pick up the forlorn woman who was holding a pair of ripped nylons and standing on the side of the road with bare, bleeding legs.

In the metaphor of my spiritual journey, that flat tire in a very strange way foreshadowed the failure to come on my pilgrimage—the slough, the mire, the getting stuck on the side of the road trying to find a way home. And although failure was a first and necessary step to getting back on the road, at the time it just made me feel like a total wreck.

Love, of course, was my first failure. I was naive about Ty, convinced that tough-muscled patience would make things work out. Men were like raccoons. If you just waited long enough, the man you were waiting for would come down out of the tree, blinking in the bright light. I had grown up under the banner mantra that says "Love Is a Choice." Interpreted one way, true love can be made, not found, and if you stick it out long enough, eventually the guy will like you back. I was wrong. *Agape* love, a Greek word every good Christian kid learns for unconditional love, is not the same as *eros* love. Mutual interest is kind of necessary. After his "let's be friends and see how it goes" talk, I saw Ty with other women and knew enough to know it was over between us.

"I'm finished with men," I said to Addison one morning. I told her that a family friend had called to set me up with some graduate student in psychology. Anticipating yet another heartbreak, I promptly rejected the idea of even meeting him. I wrote in my journal, full of postlove melodrama, "I don't believe in marriage as an opiate to human angst and alienation. The human condition is steadfast in its crisis."

"Men are a pain in the neck," Addison said.

I nodded. "Ty really burned me, or maybe I burned myself."

The night before, I had gone out with Addison and gotten drunk in my state of distress. She slept on my couch to keep me company. Somewhere between drinking and sleeping, I knelt on the linoleum floor of my kitchen sobbing like a child. I could feel my loneliness for men settling in like a darkness. But I could also feel something heavier coming up behind it, like a storm after nightfall—my deeper loneliness for God. Love and lust and spiritual longing were all mixed up together in my heart, the search for carnal love confused with the greater search for transcendent love.

I cried for probably an hour. Addison sat quietly beside me, not praying over me or giving advice, but just leaving room for my grief.

The next morning, we sat together in the living room. "You should harpoon Ty through the head," she said, trying to comfort me.

"That would be nice vindication, wouldn't it? I used to house-sit for him when he was gone. I loved him in the absence. It was some weird metaphor for our friendship that I didn't see until it was too late."

"You know what'll happen to you? You'll marry some

guy ten years older. When you're eighty and he's ninety, he'll watch TV and you'll tell jokes in front of him that he won't get. It'll be great."

"Senile love is better than no love at all."

"I have no romantic intentions. I just want to be an old putz married to an old putz."

"But how do we get from here to there?" I said in a forlorn voice. "It's a land mine. I feel so disappointed, not just with men but with everything."

In my disillusionment, I had started spending more time with my friends from work, sans Ty. Together we did things that felt useless and indulgent, like roaming around someone's apartment one night drinking wine and making a plotless amateur movie on a digital video camera. In their company, I went to parties where people smoked recreational marijuana. I went to a gay lounge called Dempsey's Brass Rail to see a drag show just for the heck of it. And I went out to bars almost every weekend.

In the same way that Damon and I used to frequent the Blue Spark, I kept company with my work colleagues at a scruffy downtown bar called Mootsie's. Until one or two in the morning, I would sit in a corner booth with a producer and his lawyer wife, a photographer who hung his motorcycle helmet on the coat rack, and a grip who brought his girlfriend of the week. An air of casual boredom marked our get-togethers. Someone at the table would pull out a pack of smokes and flick a cigarette lighter—a brief flair of light in the black expanse of a bar. The band would strike up. The cocktails would keep coming. For hours, I would drink and cuss and carry on with the rest of them.

It's hard to describe what those nights were like for me, slouched back in the booth seat and sliding a mixed drink back and forth between my hands. I felt like a different person. I wasn't talking about God and meaning. I'd stepped over the threshold and left the building. The church was behind me. The stones were gone. In front of me lay open, unmarked landscape. I felt weightless and careless.

I felt reckless too. One weekend, I drove with two work friends up to a resort town north of Spokane to attend a small film festival. After the festival, we drank way too much wine, rented a hotel room rather than drive home, and then wound up in a sexless but indulgent ménage à trois. I was like a caged wild animal that had been let out for the night. I woke up hungover the next morning and thought, Where am I? Who am I? What am I doing?

Although I felt confusion, I didn't feel anything approximating regret. Quite frankly, I was almost indifferent. I wasn't putting my body in danger by getting pregnant or doing drugs. Nothing else mattered to me. My heart was out drifting in the dark somewhere, alone and untouchable, like a kite whose kite runner had stopped watching and let the string unwind into the air. My corporeal self lived on without its moral center, its compass. I just didn't care. And although some people might see the drinking, cussing, and ménage à trois in the same way they view my teen interest in "secular" music — as pedestrian rebellion — they were for me a mark of change. I had lost myself and my way.

I felt off-course not just in my love life but in my work life too. After a year as a production assistant, I'd been drafted to work as an assistant producer in the new television division. The division at the time was dedicated in part to producing content for cable and network TV. As part of research into the new division, I attended an industry conference in New Orleans, back before the city went under water.

"Take a swamp tour for me," Damon said to me on the phone before I left, calling from his *Bennie and Joon* house. I pictured him sitting out on the dilapidated back porch, smoking a cigarette and watching the river course west.

"Forget about alligators, Damon," I said. "I'll come back traumatized by hundreds of shallow, money grubbing entertainment baboons."

"Of course you will. You're a missionary kid. Anyway, when are you going to produce your magnum opus?"

"Give me a few years. I just started this, Damon."

"I can't wait to see it, whatever it is, a documentary about a Tupperware party, I don't care."

Other people liked my job more than I did. Driven by his rampant obsession with pop and art culture, Damon thought I had been summoned to the right hand of God as a member of the entertainment industry. My father wanted my job for his love of technology—all that software, hardware, and high-end gear. My maternal grandmother, too, had an outsized idea of my work. Every time I wrote to tell her about an award or a conference event, she thought I was winning an Oscar and would send out mass family emails that I had to retract and correct.

The conference took place in downtown New Orleans at a huge complex on the banks of the Mississippi River.

Inside, the conference center ballroom was packed with television professionals trying to buy and sell program wares. In between sessions, attendees worked the selling room and took part in an elaborate courtship ritual: distributors hit on producers (vying to represent their content), producers hit on television executives (vying for support and air time), and television executives played coy with everyone. People scanned nametags to locate each other in the hierarchy of power and then conducted conversations accordingly. The whole event seemed like a high-profile, professional meat market.

The conference would have given my grandmother a heart attack. My dear mother with all of her values-laden mantras might have laughed in horror at all the shallow content. Forget about television as a distraction from books or volunteerism. It was so much more than that; television was Vanity Fair's penthouse party. Apart from a few PBS stations, most of the content being sold was sensational drama or reality television schlock, everything from sex shows to cop shows to pet shows. In one booth, a woman in heels and a strapless leopard-print dress was drinking Pepsi and promenading back and forth with a live boa constrictor wrapped around her neck—some gimmick for a cable show she was trying to sell.

Scattered on tables in the selling room were conference-sponsored publications that included industry blurbs on the mercenary battle for TV headlines. My favorite: "Car Crash Survivor Hot Network Property: Robert Ward, who after a car crash survived for six days on taco sauce and melted snow, has found himself the center of a bidding war by morning shows fighting for an exclusive interview."

The conference sessions had the same vibe as the selling room. In a discussion panel that I attended one afternoon, an industry moderator fired questions at five cable-television representatives, trying to root out their network's mission and goals.

MTV: "Really, when it comes down to it, our viewers have sex with our content. That's how we think about it. That's how we keep our viewers hooked."

E: "We're all about escapism."

The Learning Channel: "The 'learning' part of the Learning Channel is out; we're looking now for a breakout series on sex."

MTV again: "We cross-purpose for web and call it 'multiplatfornication.'"

Listening to the panel talk, I thought, Who cares about this stuff? Something had changed from when I started my job. I experienced what some tourists do when they visit a foreign city. Everything seems interesting for a while, but then the novelty wears off and you want to go home. I felt a sense of displacement. A longing for belonging. A need for purpose and calling. I was twenty-four years old. My mother at my age was teaching second graders in Philadelphia. Amy Carmichael was saving girls from the sex trade in southern India. Even my little brother was doing something more meaningful than me.

Earlier that year, Nate had gone to Sudan as a medical aid worker for a nongovernmental organization working in war-torn regions of the country. His work there seemed like the perfect fulfillment of our childhood, going back to East Africa to volunteer with an NGO in the same way that our parents had volunteered to serve with the Quakers. In his emails, Nate told stories about driving a Land Rover through landmine country on his way to a refugee camp. Picturing him off-road trying to avoid bombs, I thought to myself, *My brother is helping refugees at risk to his own life. He's making good on the great responsibility of being human. I might as well be selling Twinkies for a living.*

Late in the afternoon after sessions had ended, I walked outside the conference center and along the Mississippi River, mired in thought. In the search for love, faith, and life purpose, I was failing on all fronts and driving around with three flat tires. I felt tired of heartbreak with men. Tired of making small talk with television executives. Tired of sitting in dimly lit bars drinking cocktails with production junkies who had no interest in the dark art of ultimate meaning. In my faith life, disillusionment had cut both ways, first with the church behind me, now with the aimless space in front of me. Neither place seemed like home.

That night, my purse was stolen off the back of my bar stool while I was sitting in a jazz bar having a drink and trying to get my bearings. I spent the last day of the conference canceling credit cards and trying to avoid identity theft. After the conference, I stayed in New Orleans with some old friends and rode around on a borrowed bike for two days. I felt like Binx Bolling from Percy's *The Moviegoer.* I read novels in French Quarter cafés and bummed around bookstores and historic cemeteries.

One afternoon while riding through the city, I found myself on the front steps of an old Baptist church. Across the street from the church I saw a convenience store with bars on its windows and down the other street, a row of rental flats lined up with their leaning porches. After leaving my bike outside, I walked into the church and sat down in a pew. The sanctuary was empty inside except for a bike propped against a prayer bench in front of the altar. I hadn't been inside a church in at least a year and a half or maybe two; I couldn't even remember. As I sat there staring up at the old organ mounted on the front wall, a frail, middle-aged man came walking in from a side door.

"Hello, ma'am."

"Hello."

"Have you ever been to Ebenezer Baptist?"

"I haven't."

He introduced himself as the janitor, told me that the church dated back to 1910, and offered to show me around. I asked about the bell tower. He asked if I wanted to see it for myself. At the back of the sanctuary, I followed him up a set of narrow, rickety stairs that looked as if they were on the verge of collapse.

"Termite damage," he said.

We came out onto a small landing that circled around the bell. Off to the right was a small latched door about the size of a bathroom window.

"It goes out onto the roof," he said.

"May I go out?"

"By all means. Take your time," he said, turning back down the stairs. "There's a nice view."

I unlatched the door, crouched down, and crawled through onto a sloped roof that looked out over the entire city of New Orleans. It was windy and cold. Off in the distance, Lake Pontchartrain traced a thin line at the edge of the horizon. I sat down on the slant of the roof and pulled my hood over my head and my knees against my chest. Looking out over the city, I wondered what in my tired heart had prompted me to open the doors of a church to seek refuge.

It wasn't the first time I had done something like that. While I was in San Francisco during college, dying my hair and dancing in red-light discotheques, I walked into an Episcopal cathedral one Sunday morning and sat in a pew halfway down the sanctuary. All around me, I saw stained-glass windows ascending to the ceiling and stone buttresses arcing high overhead. When the usher invited my row up for communion, I found myself drawn forward almost involuntarily. I walked up to the front of the cathedral, knelt on the kneeling bench, and took the sacrament that was given. Then with my arms crossed over my chest and my head bowed, I felt the hand of the priest coming down upon my head to bless me. Even in my discontent with church, I wanted to be blessed. I wanted that priestly hand upon my head. And then I wanted to leave.

Chapter 15

INTO THE DARK

A few months after Ty and I went our separate ways, Michael called and told me he was coming into town for another lecture. We had dinner at a downtown restaurant as if we'd never broken things off. I went to him for sympathy and companionship, a wounded heart regressing back to the place of familiarity. After dinner, we drove back to his hotel. His room looked out over the street below. You could hear the soft sound of traffic in the background. We stayed part of the evening together, talking and seeking reprieve from the loneliness of our individual lives. I cried a few times. Lying on my side in the crumpled sheets, I said to Michael, "I feel lost."

That night, love revisited turned out to be a disappointment. Michael was a rest stop on the road. He was a place to pause but not to stay. Although I couldn't say why, I decided to leave the hotel late in the evening. I wanted to go home. After getting dressed, I said goodbye, rode the elevator to the first floor, and then drove up the hill to my apartment.

By then, my roommate had moved out and I had moved into the bedroom that she used to occupy. Her closet was empty. Her desk was gone. I had more space to myself than was probably healthy for me at the time. Feeling left behind, I took the open space as an excuse for isolation and started cutting myself further off from community. I kept in touch with Damon and Addison, but only intermittently. I saw my family only now and then and disclosed very little about my life.

Every day after work, I would come home, make dinner, and settle into an old yellow wingback chair doing the one thing I knew how to do in solitude—read books. I started revisiting books I had read in college and wanted to read again: *The Plague* by Albert Camus, *The Moviegoer* by Walker Percy, *Another Country* by James Baldwin, *The Unbearable Lightness of Being* by Milan Kundera, and Walter Kaufmann's *Existentialism from Dostoevsky to Sartre*. I went to used bookstores and bought more books. Some of them I carried with me but never got around to reading, as if having them nearby might be comfort enough. They sat in the back window of my car with their covers curling slowly in the sun like dried orange peels.

Along with reading literature, running at night became one of the rituals of my wilderness. I ran alone, despite common sense and despite emails forwarded by my grandmother in Colorado outlining all the ways in which a woman should protect herself from nighttime assailants. Watch for windowless vans. Don't sit in your car in a low-lit parking lot. If you ever get thrown in a trunk, punch out the rear headlights and wave like crazy. The "how not to get raped and pillaged" list didn't recommend jogging at night with headphones as a safe habit for women. But for me, it was the only way to exorcise my anxiety.

I took the same route almost every night, circumventing St. John's Cathedral in the soft light of the spire and then running down the streets of the neighborhood. As I ran, I often listened on my headphones to music by Radiohead, a band formed in the mid '80s by five young Oxfordshire Brits. With track titles like "Subterranean Homesick Alien" and "Paranoid Android," their albums sounded like dark existentialist literature put to song in the digital age. For me, their music was part of the history of my college awakening and, after college, a soundtrack to my solitude.

At the time, I was still writing music reviews for the weekly arts paper. I tracked music trends with religious zeal and wrote end-of-year "top ten" summations that often listed Radiohead. When the band was slated to perform at the Gorge in central Washington, I called the music editor and begged him to let me write an article promoting the upcoming concert. After he consented, I sat at the computer for hours, tapping on the keys and trying to figure out how to articulate the experience of Radiohead music. I went jogging too to get inside their songs again. In the end, what I composed was part music review, part hero worship, and part projection of my intense self-torment.

"If you can depend on anything consistent with Radiohead, you can depend on the band's sense of paradox," I wrote. "They reek of nihilism and, with their wailing, demand hope. Radiohead comes closer than most to giving angst a span of wings." After I submitted my piece, the music editor slogged through my dense prose, cut it down into something readable, and published it a week before the concert. I felt almost spiritually satisfied by the act of writing that review and seeing it in print, as if I had some-how shone a light in the shadows of my heart.

On the day of the event, I piled into a car with some friends from college and drove west through the flat farm-land of central Washington. Like good Sunday school stu-dents reviewing Bible verses on their way to church, we listened to our favorite Radiohead songs on the trip. As the Columbia River came into sight, we turned off the freeway and pulled into the parking lot of the Gorge concert venue. I had never been before. I saw an amphitheater big enough to hold twenty thousand people. Terraces led down to the concert stage. Behind the stage, the Columbia River Gorge was laid out in a dramatic expanse of rock and river and sky. The setting sun lit fire on the far side of the river in a scene that looked almost prehistoric.

Two hours later, after the sunset and after the opening music act, Radiohead came on stage. Lights illuminated the band against the night sky. An outline of the Columbia Gorge was barely visible in the distance. Huge twenty-foot screens hung on each side of the stage, projecting black-and-white images of the concert—close-ups of the lead singer's lips, the guitarist's hands, the drummer's profile.

During the concert, I didn't talk much. I felt introspec-tive and alone. My community in all its separate parts was dispersing. By then, some of my work friends had moved to Los Angeles to make their names as filmmakers. Ty had packed up his little house and moved west over the moun-tains to Seattle. Damon was getting ready to move back to the Bay Area. My other college peers—those attending the Radiohead concert—had applied to graduate schools. The few friendships I had seemed transient, connections being pulled apart by change, time, and distance.

In that disconsolate space, I watched my favorite band perform. The concert went on for hours. Toward the end, I decided to venture into the mosh pit. I felt as if I were going forward at a tent revival meeting, moved by some unnamed urge to enter the fray and be touched by the fire. I didn't tell anyone I was going. I just got up and walked down the steep hill to the stage.

Packed tight, the people in the mosh pit weren't drunk with adrenaline the way they often are at rock concerts. They swayed back and forth, almost in meditation. At the far corner stood a security guard whose job was less to calm the crowd and more to help people in and out. The pit was impossible to navigate alone or on foot. After watching how other concertgoers made their way in, I walked up to the security guard, who lifted me off my feet and then vaulted me face down onto the top of the crowd. I felt myself being carried by hands into the middle of the mosh pit, a community of strangers who held me aloft like a levitating body.

When I was about fifty feet in, they let me down gently. Standing again, I looked to find my bearings and saw only five feet in front of me the stage edge and the entire band almost within arm's reach. The members of a band I'd listened to for years—Thom Yorke and Jonny Greenwood and Ed O'Brien—were right there in the flesh. I could feel the heat from the burning stage lights. It was glorious. Right then, I experienced the religious euphoria that I'd seen on television in the Clapton concert. This time, I was *in* the concert audience. I was the one transfixed and taken

in, listening to music as prophecy, as memory, as the fulfillment of some mysterious spiritual longing.

But then the moment changed. Staring at the lead
singer and watching him watch us—thousands of people
who'd come to see their hero perform live—I saw something on his face that I'll never forget. His expression
seemed almost unmistakable to me. I saw the alienation of a
rock star icon who knew he couldn't give the deliverance we
wanted. He disdained us for turning him into a god. While
I stood there in front of the stage, my awe changed into disappointment. I felt like a mountain climber who hikes up
a high peak and then finds a higher peak behind it. Even
music could be a source of dissatisfaction on the search, if I
asked too much of it.

I watched the lead singer for a few minutes. Then, overwhelmed with loneliness in the company of thousands, I
raised my arms high into the air. A raised hand was the sign
for departure. The crowd lifted me up, turned me face
down onto the surface, and carried me out to the edge of
the bright stage. There, the security guard let me back on
my feet and back into the dark.

PART SIX

THE HILL DIFFICULTY

On his way up to the House Beautiful,
Pilgrim has to climb the hill called Difficulty.
Both the hill and the road up are called
Difficulty.

Chapter 16

A STRANGE, INSIPID BEER PARTY

Me with Will's snake, Voltaire

One night after coming home from work, I rummaged through my cupboard for dinner and got hit in the head with a can of refried beans that fell off the top shelf when I wasn't looking. I took it as a sign and ate the beans with cheese in a tortilla. Standing alone in my kitchen with my paper plate and pathetic dinner, I thought, Being young feels like crap. Addison had once said to me, laughing darkly, "Sometimes I just want to go to church camp and be converted. I want to be slain in the Spirit, then go out to Perkins for French fries." We both knew finding our way was not that easy. The search seemed lonely and confusing. Sometimes you found yourself eating canned beans in a small, cold kitchen.

After dinner, I pulled off my bookshelf Hermann Hesse's *Steppenwolf,* which I was reading as part of my foray into existentialist literature. The book inspired the crazy '60s rock band and also inspired part of my father's search back in the early '70s. The main character in the story struggles to reconcile his animal self (an alienated wolf) with his transcendent self and feels caught between misery and hope. The cover illustration of my paperback copy showed a man hunched over and walking down a cobblestone road, another Pilgrim on his sad pilgrim way.

That night, I read the first two chapters of the book. Then I plowed through the third. As I read, I sensed an undeniable despair coming over me. To some, it may sound strange and slightly indulgent that I was moved so much by a novel. But for me, it marked a significant juncture on my path. I was lost.

The despair I felt reminded me of a dream that I had around the time that I left the church. In it, I was driving after dusk through wooded countryside trying to find a grotto where priests served Living Water for those who were thirsty. A friend had told me about the place. The water was supposed to cure anything, renew anyone, and give blessing to those in need. I found the grotto, a cave with stone walls and a fire in the hearth. Men in Benedictine robes were serving guests with white porcelain pitchers of water. After I arrived, one of the robed priests took me to a table where I sat with an empty cup. I waited for water. I waited for hours. But no one came. After a while, it became apparent that no one was coming. I remember that moment almost as if it were a real experience, not a dream. I felt completely abandoned. I was thirsty and alone. Looking around the room one last time, I stood up, stepped through the doorway, and walked out into the night.

Reading *Steppenwolf* elicited the same feeling for me. I felt lost and alienated. I sensed God's absence not in a dream but in a lucid waking moment. Although it's hard for me to know how to say this, I thought about suicide for the first time in my life that night. I didn't exactly feel the desire to kill myself. I felt the desire to *die*. In the abstract, it seemed like a relief. A way out of the woods. Every day, I was going to work in a rote way, running in the dark, and then milling around my apartment in a mire of confusion. I was isolated more than ever and trapped in my own search. With *Steppenwolf* laying open on my lap, I looked at my front door and thought, How do I escape?

Then a strange thing happened. Almost as if summoned, someone knocked on the door. The knocking came lightly, like the tapping of an apparition on the other side of the wall. I unlocked the security chain and opened the door, half expecting to see God incarnate on the other side. It was Will, standing there with Voltaire draped over his shoulder as if it were perfectly normal to knock on someone's door while carrying a pet reptile.

"You're wearing purple," he said, noticing the color of my shirt. He didn't notice my face—I'd been crying—and somehow I was relieved by his oversight.

"Can I borrow some sugar?" he said. "Jess is making muffins." Jess was his roommate.

"Sure, come on in." Will followed me into the kitchen, petting Voltaire in an aimless way as he talked.

"My brother the other day, he calls and tells me his wife has cancer. Can you believe it?"

"I'm so sorry, that's horrible."

"He has two kids."

As Will talked, I reached up into the top cupboard above my stove and pulled down the granulated sugar. I poured two cups into a plastic bag and handed it to him as we walked back into the living room. Standing on the threshold, Will said, "Do you want to come up and eat muffins with us?"

"No thanks, Will."

After shutting the door, I scrolled through my cell phone directory trying to find someone to call. Will had knocked me out of my despair just long enough to make me realize that I had much less to complain about than someone diagnosed with cancer. I needed to get up and move. I needed a friend to talk to, someone I had known for a long time. I tried calling a friend in San Francisco. No answer. I tried a friend in Seattle. No answer. Then, instead of calling someone in the city where I lived, I walked down the stairs to the carport and got into my car with the intent of finding someone, anyone, who was home. I had spent so many nights driving around trying to find solitude and escape, and now, suddenly, I was driving around trying to find community.

I went all over the city, slowing down to pass by the house of one friend and the apartment of another. No one was home. I drove for half an hour until finally I found an old friend from my childhood church with her living room lights on. Pulling up in front of her house, I parked the car and walked up onto the porch. Moths circled the light overhead. I opened the screen and knocked on the door. On the other side, I could hear the sound of footsteps on wood floors, coming closer.

"What brings you?" Cathy said, opening the door.

"I'm lonely. May I come in?"

"Of course."

Cathy was a member of Knox and an old family friend who had known me for almost twenty years. She worked at a cemetery and helped bury people for a living. She was also one of the middle-aged women in my life that I counted not as a mentor but as a friend—someone I could go to a wine bar with and divulge the troubles of my life. When Michael and I had been involved, I had gone to Cathy. Ty too. She had listened to me and talked about her own story.

As I stepped into her living room that night, I saw her teenage son watching *The Simpsons* and chasing the cat around during a commercial break. Her eldest daughter was whining about wanting to go to Walmart. Her husband was changing a lightbulb in the bedroom.

"Come sit," Cathy said. She handed me a glass of wine and folded her legs beneath her on the couch as we sat down.

"I like to stand among the dead," she said. "They don't

say, 'I'm bored. What's to eat? Take me to Walmart.' They don't make any racket."

She made me laugh, and when I laughed I felt myself relax. The candle Cathy had lit on the fireplace mantle when I first arrived burned down slowly as we talked and drank wine. Her husband finished putting in the lightbulb and eventually left to take their daughter to Walmart. Her son came and went from the living room, watching TV and running into the kitchen after the cat. The phone in the dining room rang now and then and went to voicemail.

For the two hours that I stayed at Cathy's house that night, I didn't talk about anything personal. I didn't cry or bare my heart. Watching the routine motions of a family gave me comfort and in some way made me completely forget about myself. When it was time for Cathy to go to bed for her morning shift at the cemetery, she helped me with my coat and stood on the porch with the light on until I was in my car turning over the engine.

On the way back to my apartment, I watched the road in front of me from the quiet space of my car. By then fall had set in and maple trees were drying and turning color. The leaves on the boulevards lifted up like birds being flushed out in the rush of traffic. While driving home, I felt peace for the first time in a long time. My burden eased. A shadow lifted.

■ ■ ■

A few weeks after he came down to borrow sugar, Will came down at ten o'clock again one night and knocked on my door. When I opened it, he was standing there with a beer in his hand and Voltaire wrapped around his neck haphazardly like a live winter scarf.

"What time are you going to bed?"

"I don't know. Why?"

"My friend who lives in Guatemala is visiting. You should meet her. We're having a party."

I paused.

"Sure, I'll come up."

Will brought me in through the kitchen door of his apartment as if I were an old friend. The last time I'd been in his kitchen, I had crawled through the garbage door. While Will stood at the sink getting me a glass of water, I noticed that on his cupboards he'd taped pictures ripped from magazines, at least half a dozen photos of human suffering and exploitation.

On the cabinet next to the sink hung a picture of a Walmart truck with the caption, "Plenty of gas, plenty of pay, and plenty of bombs to keep it this way." Another photo showed a starving child in the arms of its helpless mother. The caption read, "Every four seconds a child dies after a long period of suffering from starvation that could have been prevented with an amount of money that most Americans wouldn't pick up if they saw it laying in the road." He had other starving-baby pictures too. They were the sorts of images you flip past when looking through a magazine at the doctor's office—photos you can only bear to look at once, let alone every time you open the cupboard to pull out the peanut butter.

"What are these?" I asked.

"I want to remember," he said, "how other people live. What my choices mean."

I was so taken by what he said, the conscience of a lackluster, slow-moving, bangs-in-the-eyes boy. I had misjudged Will. Standing in his kitchen right then, the Quaker missionary kid in me felt a sudden friendship with him. He understood the burden of comparative living — always remembering other people's circumstances, always remembering other people's needs.

That night as I sat on Will's couch making small talk with his friend from Guatemala and a few others, Will and I ended up getting into a philosophical repartee about the existence of God. Will slouched on the couch in his usual fashion, Voltaire draped over his shoulder and a Coors cupped in his left hand.

"Do you believe in God?" He asked me almost out of nowhere.

Without hesitating, I said, "Yes, why?"

"Just curious." He took a sip from his beer. "Do you believe morality is objective or subjective?"

"Depends. I think morality is practiced subjectively and differently in different cultures, but that we all share the same fundamental moral wiring: don't kill, don't steal, don't cheat, that kind of thing. The framework is objective." I paused. "What do *you* think?"

"I think morals are totally subjective; therefore God is unnecessary."

I knew this move. It was a move that didn't work for someone who had taped up magazine pictures with implicit moral messages. Full of adrenaline and talking with my hands, I said, "But, if morals are totally subjective, then you can't say Hitler was wrong. You can't say there's anything unjust about letting babies starve. And you can't condemn evil. How tenable is that?" Will shifted in his seat and kept listening.

"You have to consent to an objective moral standard, up here." I waved my hand in a high horizontal line. "And if you consent to an objective moral standard, then justice has a mooring point, and the possibility of a divine moral mind comes into play."

By then, I had stood up off the couch and was almost preaching. The people around us were talking, drinking, and lounging on the ratty furniture in the living room. As Will grinned at me with curiosity, I wondered why I was trying so hard to convince my beer-buzzed neighbor that God exists. I dreamt about despair. But somewhere in a place deeper than those dreams, I believed in meaning. I believed that the urge against darkness meant there was light. More than that, I believed in God. And now I was hearing myself say it, in the middle of a strange, insipid beer party. It didn't matter if my ideas held up to scrutiny. It mattered that I was arguing for theism, the first step in faith, at a time in my life when I had stepped away from the church.

Sitting back down on Will's couch after my rant as the skeptical apologist, I thought, Something's changed. In hindsight, I can say more accurately that almost nothing had changed. My deep, inescapable beliefs had only been pushed underground for a time and were now beginning to emerge again, like plant bulbs that go dormant for a while and then grow back. What prompted the change was hard to say. "Like a whispering in dark streets," wrote the poet Rilke, "rumors of God run through your dark blood."

We had more conversations after that, Will and I. Sometimes in the evening after work, I would trudge upstairs and find Will out on the back stoop behind our apartment building. I started taking comfort in his presence. He knew nothing about me and nothing about my Christian childhood or my conflicted heart. He was neutral and safe and pleasantly indifferent to me, the droopy college boy who drew blood at the hospital and sat on the back porch smoking cheap cigarettes with his pet snake wrapped around his arm. I could always find him there. Together, we talked about the philosophy of mathematics — was math discovered or invented, and what did that say about the nature of the universe? We talked about some weird paper he was writing for school about slugs. We talked about proofs for God's existence, moral and otherwise. And we talked about how God was always at the edge of our knowing.

I journaled a lot during that time, sometimes while sitting on the back porch with Will. He would study his school textbooks and I would scribble in my spiral-bound notebook, drawing a series of amateur philosophical maps that I used to try to make sense of my questions. The maps had arrows and shorthand fragments that I can hardly make sense of now: "Complaint of lack of goodness/beauty posits existence of ideal (in goodness/beauty) → leads to ... [unreadable] → indicative of belief in nonnatural world/ God, [unreadable], etc."

During our conversation in Kenya, Jerry had talked about the problem of good. I couldn't really hear what he had to say at the time. Two years later it started to mean something to me. As a counterpoint to the problem of evil, the problem of good was part of what I'd been trying to say to Will at his beer party and part of what I was trying to work out in my journaling. Something good like justice couldn't be meaningless—it had to have origin and purpose—and something beautiful like music couldn't be meaningless, either. If, however, life was a cosmic accident, then justice didn't exist. Art was an expression of white noise. But even the members of Pink Floyd, Will's favorite band, seemed as if they were pointing at something. They felt longing, didn't they? Wasn't it possible they were pushing toward God without knowing it?

Had I lived next door to Will and not beneath his mammoth stereo system, I might have learned to like Pink Floyd for all their sad, searching riffs. As it was, I never did. Will had his search to undertake. I had mine. He moved out a few years after I moved in. I never saw him again. I still have one of his CDs that I forgot to return to him, by an '80s band self-consciously called "The The." The album, called "Infected," shows a round crablike monster on the cover and a planet in orbit over a cityscape. I have no idea what it means.

I never knew Will's last name. He was both a stranger and a friend. When he moved out, I missed him in an odd way as someone who represented the start of my turn back home. He became the boy upstairs who helped me remember how I saw the world and the world-beyond-the-world, the great mystery of faith and goodness and God.

Chapter 17

TAKING MY DEMONS TO CHURCH

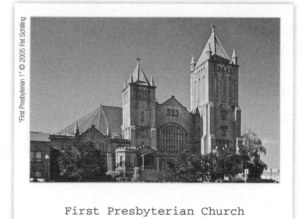

First Presbyterian Church

For Halloween that fall, Damon, up visiting from the Bay Area, dressed as Charlie Chaplin and came over to my apartment to hand out candy to kids and make homemade donuts in my kitchen. For two hours, we ate donuts, listened to Mahalia Jackson on the stereo, and waited for a door knock until we realized that most parents don't take their kids through apartment buildings on Halloween.

"I want to direct another Beckett play at my dad's church," Damon said. We were sitting next to each other on my futon couch. "Which one should I do?"

"Kill Samuel Beckett," I said, throwing my arms in the air and tossing donut crumbs on the floor. "I'm tired of Beckett, he's obsessed with despair. It's like listening to Depeche Mode's lead singer still singing about teen angst at age forty."

"You're a heretic!"

I smiled. "You'll kill me, won't you, defecting from Beckett like this?"

"Absolutely. Heresy has to be punished."

"But don't you get it? There's territory beyond despair, something just as profound, but it's beautiful and goes on for miles, and why didn't Beckett at least point to it?"

"Maybe he did."

"If everything's meaningless, then why make art? He made art. So maybe it was a nihilist's subversive way of pointing at meaning."

"His inside joke," Damon said.

"I've started going to church again, Damon," I said, changing the subject. The last song on the Mahalia Jackson CD had finished, leaving a noticeable quiet.

"Say a prayer for me, sister, for this old depraved soul." Damon chuckled and leaned forward on his Charlie Chaplin cane.

"I don't know why, but I want to try it, at least. I think I'm working out my demons."

"You'll always have demons."

"Yes, I'll always have demons. But I might as well take my demons to church."

A few weeks before, on a quiet Sunday morning, I had gotten up, eaten breakfast, and gone to church for the first time in two years. I went to First Presbyterian, a huge, thousand-member church in downtown Spokane near the I-90 freeway, which cuts across Washington State. I passed its stone spires every time I drove west. After parking my car, I walked up the stairway into the sanctuary and sat in the back row alone. Although I saw a few familiar faces in the congregation — friends of my parents, former Whitworth students, some of my dad's medical students — I spoke to no one and left right after the service.

The next Sunday, I ran into a family friend who worked as the church organist and found myself sitting in the very front row. Above me, organ pipes circled the front of the sanctuary. Beneath them I saw a grand piano and next to it, the organ. Getting down from the organ and then handing me a hymnal as she stood beside me in the pew, the organist seemed neutral and safe the way Will did while sitting with me on the back porch. She didn't know my story. She didn't know that I hadn't been to church for two years. She was just a friend to me for that hour.

After the service had ended, I ran into the man who had pastored Knox for a few years while I was in college. We talked for a few minutes and then a friend of his came up to say hi. He turned out to be the graduate student that my family friend had tried to set me up with during my post-Ty sanction on men. He seemed smart and interesting.

231

Standing there with both of them in a crowd of congre-gants, I thought, If these are the kinds of people who go here, maybe I might be able to give this a try. I was dating the church again, taking it one step at a time and trying to feel things out.

After attending First Presbyterian for about four months, I took a risk and decided to go back to the church of my childhood. One Sunday morning, I got in my car and drove down the hill to Knox and Post. Walking up to the front door, I was invited in by a man who had been the greeter since I was a child, a funny retiree who made faces at kids and lifted old widows into the elevator chair that hummed up the stairs onto the landing. He greeted me as if I'd been going to church every Sunday of my life without fail.

For me, though, going back to Knox was like going back to see an old friend that I'd been estranged from for years. I felt nervous and anxious. I felt nostalgic too, walking into the sanctuary and seeing the pews where I'd sat for fifteen years of my life, the pulpit where the pastors had preached, and the stage where youth interns had performed their campy VBS skits every summer. About halfway down, I saw my parents in the same place they'd sat for the last twenty years of their church attendance.

At first, I stayed at the back of the sanctuary in the same place the bride stands before she walks down the aisle and commits her life to someone. Then, after holding back for a moment, I went forward and sat with my parents as if it was a perfectly normal thing to do. They tried hard not to register shock that their daughter was back at church.

"Please rise for the doxology," the pastor said. He held

his robe-draped arms out toward the congregation to bring us to our feet for the singing of the doxology, "From Whom All Blessings Flow." The whole service was still familiar to me—the liturgy, the prayers, the sacrament of communion. Even my parents' habits were the same. My mother penciled notes in her bulletin. My father nodded at notable insights in the sermon. I sat next to them for the duration of the service, taking it all in.

In the geography of my spiritual story, I had returned to the threshold of the church and was standing looking in rather than out. What prompted my return seemed as mysterious as my departure. I left for a while, burned out by faith and church. Then I came back, driven by a completely different kind of fatigue. I was tired of myself. Tired of being an overwrought, introspective twentysomething trying to undertake the search alone. But even in my homecoming, I felt both clarity and confusion. Wondering if I'd come back too soon, I thought, Am I ready to be back at church?

"After the accident," Jerry had said to me once, "I went to church again, but I couldn't bring myself to sing the hymns. I let other people sing for me. I let them carry me." I pictured him standing in a dark mahogany pew of First Presbyterian surrounded by churchgoers and staring up at the tall organ pipes while the congregation sang an old nineteenth-century hymn. I pictured him present and absent at the same time, standing but not singing. Jerry's story wasn't anything like mine, but I understood the feeling of ambivalence that he described in going back to church.

At the end of the service that Sunday, the pastor held out his arms again and said, "Please rise and join hands for

FAITH AND OTHER FLAT TIRES

our final hymn, number 690 in your pew hymnals." No one opened their hymnals. Everyone knew the song by heart. By tradition on communion Sunday, the congregation held hands in a long unbroken chain and sang the hymn "Bind Us Together." My parents stood up first. After a brief hesitation, I stood up too and began singing along. I held my mother's hand on one side and the hand of a stranger on the other.

> Bind us together, Lord,
> Bind us together,
> With cords that cannot be broken.
> Bind us together Lord, Bind us together Lord,
> Bind us together with love.

A skeptical philosopher like Nietzsche, had he been sitting beside me that day, might have told me I was caving in to group pressure. "The herd," he would scratch in pencil on the side of the bulletin before passing it back to me in the middle of the sermon. Leaning forward from the pew behind, Karl Marx would have whispered in my ear that I was succumbing to religion as "the opiate of the masses," avoiding the admission that my belief was just a bourgeoisie myth used to control the populace. God was like a drug. A temporary fix. An escape from reality. At coffee hour after church, while sipping lukewarm coffee, Freud might have sauntered up to tell me that, given my unresolved sexual frustrations — not to mention issues with my father — it was no wonder I had taken up religion again. The church and I were polar magnets. Eventually, after straining for so long to pull away, I would snap back into place. Faith was something I couldn't shake, like the glue residue that stayed after I scraped the Ichthus off my Plymouth hatchback.

But then, if Nietzsche, Marx, and Freud had said those things to me, I would have cornered them all at coffee hour. Even in my ambivalence about church, I would tell them, I could sense in my heart a strong longing for God. Frederick Buechner said, "Faith is homesickness." That was how it felt to me. If we were accidents of a godless universe, I would ask, then why did I sense this enduring pull toward God, the Alpha, the Omega, the Unmoved Mover? Why did I have a soul and a mind with rational faculties? Didn't it all *mean* something?

I knew from my Western civilization course in college that Plato believed in the Forms — unchanging, eternal ideas written into the human being. We lose these ideas in the trauma of birth, he said, and spend the rest of our lives trying to recover what we lost. God, too, seemed like something lost that I was trying to find again.

To me, longing for God was like hearing music from an open window on the street or seeing mountains off in the distance. The yearning felt almost like grief. A cry born into my heart before the human heart ever existed. A desire so deep and far back that it seemed almost prehistoric. I sensed the *imago Dei*, the image of God within me. I was Plato's child searching for the lost language of my origins. I was a homing bird traveling with my outspread wings, carried by an innate compass and crossing a thousand miles to get back to the place where I began.

Even disbelief, I would tell them, was part of my search for God. Doubt impelled faith over a lifetime. Doubt was born from disappointment, disappointment was born of longing, and longing was born of the *imago Dei*. C. S. Lewis, in his preface to *Pilgrim's Regress*, says, "The human soul was made to enjoy some object that is never fully given—nay, cannot even be imagined as given—in our present mode of subjective and spatiotemporal experience."

If that was true, then this too was true. While I stood singing a hymn in an old Presbyterian church, feeling the start of a deep, uneasy peace, my doubt *was* my desire—to touch the untouchable. To possess the presence of God.

PART SEVEN

THE HOUSE BEAUTIFUL

Atop the Hill of Difficulty, Pilgrim finds the House Beautiful, a palace that serves as a rest stop for pilgrims on their way to the Celestial City. The House Beautiful is an allegory of the local Christian congregation. Its name derives from a gate of the Jerusalem temple.

Chapter 18

CAT LITTER AND NAIL POLISH

One Saturday evening, my mother called and invited me to come home for a dinner of roast and potatoes. Over dinner, my father in his usual fashion embarked on life reflections that started with a story about some heroin addict he'd seen while going on rounds at the hospital. She was a stubborn middle-aged woman tied up to IVs in her bed, swearing she didn't have what it took to quit, swearing she would rather die alone in some back alley from her last draw of "black tar" than throw her skull against the padded walls of a rehab unit.

Along with his medical residents, my dad had stood by her bedside once a day all week long talking about rehab and getting her off heroin. When it came time to release her from the hospital, she hung her head as my father left the room. He turned back, put his hand on top of her hands and said, "The Lord is your shepherd," while tears rolled down her cheeks.

"I'll quit, I'll quit," she said.

"I believe you," my dad said.

Out in the hallway after their exchange with the patient, a medical resident asked, "You don't *really* believe her, do you?"

"I do believe her. She needs someone to believe in her," he said. And then quoting the love chapter, 1 Corinthians 13, he said, "Love believes all things, hopes all things, endures all things."

In between bites of potatoes, my father told the story as evidence not of his virtue but of the transformative power of Christian love.

"Really, you believed her?" I asked incredulously.

"In the sense of hoping for her, yes, I did."

"Let me read you a passage from Dostoevsky," he said, setting down his wine glass before walking over to the bookshelf. My parents by then had revised their list of taboos. My mother rescinded her ban on sunglasses and both my parents drank wine in the evenings. But my dad still did family time every night without fail, an activity that even then, as an adult, still reminded me of being a teenager tied down to the dinner table. Some things never changed. Dinnertime couldn't just be dinnertime. We had to talk about drug addiction and redemption.

Pulling off *The Brothers Karamazov*, my dad flipped through and read aloud the passage that says, "Love in action is a harsh and dreadful thing compared to love in dreams." Then he talked about how love, and specifically *Christian* love, is a mundane and difficult act that is all the more meaningful for its difficulty. Loving others takes guts and patience.

"But don't you think Christianity suffers from hyperoptimism?" I asked.

"Ah, but that's what's so compelling about Christianity. You believe people can change. You have hope that a woman on heroin can find her life again, and that it's worth finding. You hope on her behalf. You speak into the void."

As my dad talked, he seemed inspired by and sure of his faith. Maybe I envied him for that certainty. I don't know. I was still trying to find my way back inside the church, making progress on my own terms and taking it one step at a time. On Sundays I had started going regularly to Knox. And on Tuesdays I had started attending a Bible study, of all things.

At first, I hated the idea of Bible study. It seemed dull, clean-cut, and conservative. A friend of mine from college had once invited me to join her Bible study, around the time that I started drifting from the church. "Maybe," I said in response. What I really meant was, "Over my dead body." When that same friend invited me again two years later, I felt closed to the idea and open to it at the same time. *If* I'm going to go, I thought, I should go to a study that's taught by a philosopher and not some Bible-thumping nut head.

I knew who led the Bible study. When I was a freshman in college, before I became an English major, I hung out with a group of guys who lived in an apartment off campus. They were the kind of hardy Christian boys who went to chapel, wrestled with each other, and played football in the field outside their apartment. They had a roommate named Steve, the nerdy, well-humored type who would come into the kitchen to eat a donut off the counter, crack a joke, and then retreat back into his bedroom to study his philosophy books.

On my second visit to Knox after being gone for two years, I walked into the sanctuary foyer and saw Steve standing there with a bulletin in his hand. I hadn't seen him in years and asked how he was doing. "I'm just a guy, trying to get by," he said. His comment was the sort of thing you might hear in the Midwest from a carefree man standing in a sunlit field with a piece of straw between his teeth. He seemed warm and human. While talking with him that morning, I didn't so much notice him as an available date; he just seemed like a man who might be interesting to know. He was getting his master's in philosophy from a local Jesuit university, I knew, and led the Bible study in his free time.

On the first night of the study, I went to my living room bookshelf and instead of pulling off *Steppenwolf*, slid off the NIV Bible that had sat untouched for years. Its broken spine had been bandaged with duct tape. The slips of paper with the questions from my junior high Sunday school students were still stuck inside the beseeching book of Psalms, the same place I had put them years ago.

After carpooling with my friend out to a house near Whitworth, I walked in the door carrying my Bible and saw Steve sitting on the floor talking with a guy from India who, I learned later, worked for a venture capital firm. I sat down on the floor on the other side of the room and watched them from a distance as they talked and threw back their heads now and then to laugh about something I couldn't hear. Probably ten or fifteen people were there, all post-college twentysomethings working various jobs or studying in graduate school. They seemed at peace with themselves in a way that I didn't.

"Who's read *The Brothers Karamazov?*" Steve asked at the start of the study. He led the study like a graduate student would, using interpretive commentaries as secondary sources and asking seminar-style questions. We were talking about 1 Peter and the subject of human suffering. In that context, he quoted from memory the same quote that my father had read during family time.

"It's only one translation of the text from Russian, so keep that in mind," he said. "But what does Dostoevsky mean, exactly, that love in action is a harsh and dreadful thing compared to love in dreams?"

People talked for a while about the Dostoevsky passage and its connection to 1 Peter. Someone read the verse from chapter 1 that says, "Love one another deeply, from the heart." Then Steve told a story about a friend of his who had grown up in an abusive home. "She said to me once, 'I've been entrusted with this pain.'" He paused, then added, "In context of 1 Peter, what does it mean to be entrusted with pain?"

During the ongoing discussion, I didn't say much. I felt out of place. But I also felt at home. Being around people who'd grown up in the church made me feel content in the same way a person far from home feels suddenly content when they run into someone who grew up in the same town. You mean you're from Salem, Oregon, too? What side of town did you live on? What street? As I listened to Steve, in particular, I began to see him not just as a graduate student and a study leader but as a man who lived in the same sojourning space as me. He seemed like a pilgrim on the road searching for God.

It sounds almost cliché, but I developed a crush on my Bible study leader that night. Like someone who eats too many pieces of chocolate cake, I took interest in the sandwich, finally, which wasn't a boring bologna sandwich after all but a healthy turkey sandwich. I thought to myself, Who *is* this person? But wait, I thought, I'm not the kind of woman who gets a crush on a Christian man. This is not cool.

Then again, I wasn't the same person anymore.

"I think I'm ready for a normal man," I said to Addison on the phone later, referring to my past attraction to tragic artist types. She was always the one I talked to about my trouble with men. "I need to get married. My libido is the size of a library."

"You need a pet or a roommate. Or maybe you need a roommate you can pet."

I laughed. "I'm done with missionary dating, these suffering men that I keep trying to save. It's been so dysfunctional. *I've* been so dysfunctional."

"Rule of thumb: if he's kind, he's probably boring," Addison said, trying to lighten me up, "and if he's good looking, he's probably a womanizer."

I laughed again. "I just want to love and be loved, not even in the romantic sense, you know? The whole world— it's so sad. What am I saying?"

In college, I had read the poem "Late Fragment" by Raymond Carver:

And did you get what
you wanted from this life, even so?
I did.

And what did you want?
To call myself beloved, to feel myself
beloved on the earth.

"What we go home to at the end of the day is all we have, really," I said. "I want to go home to a good man. Maybe that's what I'm trying to say."

■ ■ ■

Every week at Bible study, I started studying Steve more closely than I studied my New Testament. I scrutinized everything about him, even his fashion sensibilities. Although good-looking, he was the kind of man who spent all his cash on books and never on clothes. He wore fleece vests and geeky pleated khakis that made me cringe. He acted shy sometimes, and had acne scars that made his skin look rough. And yet for all those imperfections, I found myself drawn to his kindness, his intellect, his calm.

For months, I saw Steve not just at Bible study on Tuesdays but at Knox every Sunday. We spent time with mutual friends too. After I told Cathy the funeral director about my tentative dating interest, she started inviting Steve and me over to her house, like Yente the matchmaker from *Fiddler on the Roof,* having us over for Sabbath brunch. I didn't mind it, actually. One afternoon after church, she had me over for pizza along with Steve and my parents. A few weeks later she invited Steve and me over again to eat lunch and play baseball in the park with her husband and kids.

As if prompted by Cathy's Yente-like powers of subtle

persuasion, Steve called one night and invited me out to a movie. On my first date with my Bible study crush, I sat in a theater making small talk that turned into a lesson on Steve's dry, unpredictable humor. I didn't know much about his past, except that he'd grown up in southeast Alaska hunting and flying bush planes.

"What do your parents do?" I said.

"My mom's retired. She worked for the Alaska State Department of Transportation." Then he said, "My dad owns the second largest sweatshop in Brazil."

After a deliberate pause, he smiled wryly. I turned red with the embarrassment of an eager, gullible date who'd had her buttons pushed by someone who knew how to push buttons.

After the film, Steve drove me back to my apartment in a blue Honda hatchback that reminded me of the Plymouth I de-Ichthused during college. As I stepped into the passenger seat, Steve apologized for having a dirty car.

"Don't worry about it," I said. "I wouldn't trust anyone with a clean car."

My older brother had once told me he would judge the men I dated by their cars. If a guy's car seemed too expensive and too clean, he wouldn't pass. Real men, men with mission and purpose beyond the material world, drove dirty cars with dents and bangs and broken AC. They drove beat-up Ford Escorts or used Hondas.

"I see you have a book by Alvin Plantinga," Steve said, pulling a book off the shelf in my apartment after we arrived. I was in the kitchen making Kenyan tea.

"Honestly I've only read parts of it. The content is pretty

dense," I said, referring to a book called *God and Other Minds* by a well-known Christian philosopher from Notre Dame. A friend from college who had gone off to study analytic philosophy at UCLA had given it to me. "I like the title more than anything. It gives me confidence knowing that smart Christian philosophers are out there trying to make sense of my intellectual questions about the universe. Do you know the book?" I asked.

I handed Steve his tea and pointed to a rocking chair. I sat opposite in my yellow wingback chair and listened to Steve as he talked about the book and about arguments for the rationality of Christian belief. He seemed like the kind of person who would date a solidly Christian girl and not someone like me.

Like a woman revealing her past as a test, I said to him out of nowhere, "I stopped going to church for a couple of years. I had a lot of questions. I've only just started coming back."

"I knew that about you," he said. I was surprised at how casual and unreactionary he seemed.

"You did?"

He nodded. "You seem like the kind of person who asks deep questions, who doesn't settle for the status quo."

"I don't regret leaving church for a few years. I think I needed time to work things out. I needed a break."

Religion and politics are the two things people say you should never talk about on a first date, but for hours that night, Steve and I drank tea and covered both of those topics—especially religion. He listened to my story without evaluation, without judgment. He seemed unfazed by my disclosure of doubt. By then, the stones that had dropped out of my heart for a while I had picked up again. My questions meant something to me. I valued them. In that sense, I felt like a twelve-year-old with a rock collection who discovers that the boy next door really knows his rocks and studies them every day while sitting on the back stoop after supper. We had the search in common.

After he left, I lay in bed in the dark, wide awake from three cups of black Kenyan tea and going over the contours of our conversation like a blind woman remembering a face with her hands.

■ ■ ■

I saw Steve at church the next morning. He was teaching Sunday school at Knox. Down in the fellowship hall, I sat at a table with Scott Edminster and his wife and for the duration of the class tried not to seem too eager in my attention to the man behind the podium. Steve lectured on Holy Land archeology, showing us slides of what was alleged to be Saint Peter's house, text excerpts from the Roman historian Tacitus, ancient Herodian coins, and Galilean fishing boats.

After class, Steve and I sat together during the service. We shared a hymnal, which according to a friend of mine was a form of Christian flirting. Walking down the aisle behind him on our way to communion, I paid more attention to him than I did the sacrament. We parted ways in the parking lot after the church service was over.

As I was getting into my car, Steve pulled up beside me

in his Honda, popped open the passenger door, and asked if I wanted to come with him to visit a friend. I gathered up my skirt and climbed in. I had no idea where we were going or who we were going to visit.

"Thanks for Sunday school," I said.

Steve pulled out of the parking lot. "What did you think of it?"

"I thought it was interesting. But I had one question for you."

"Shoot."

In some fiction, I said, the author often based the events on real people and places. But it didn't follow that the narrative was true. I knew by genre that the story itself, although based on hard, empirically provable facts, was fiction. "Couldn't you make the same argument for the writings of the New Testament," I said, "that it's embellished fact?"

Steve by now had turned onto the I-90 freeway, driving east toward the mountains. He thought for a second, slipping his hands along the wheel as he drove the bends in the road.

"People take evidence, textual, historical, archeological evidence," he said, "and they try to use that to *prove* the truth of the New Testament, but that's stretching the evidence too far. We have to look at a range of evidence—archeology, the internal characteristics of the New Testament, the dates of writing—and then make the standard historical assessment. They tell us that the New Testament is *as* credible or more than any ancient document. It has just as much supportive evidence and more than other ancient documents from the same period."

"How far does that get you, then?" I asked.

"Having a credible document doesn't establish that the historical claims are true, but it does show us that it's *as* rational to believe the historical events in the New Testament as the events outlined in other sources. Historical evidence gets you one step of the way, but not all the way. It has to be part of a bigger picture, including a discussion about miracles."

"Interesting," I said. "I'll have to think more about it."

Steve bent to the side of the steering wheel then and casually turned on the radio.

"Do you know this song?"

"No, I don't."

"It's a song by Foreigner. They're the British band that did 'Cold as Ice.'"

"Are they '80s?"

"More '70s to '80s than '80s." He drummed the wheel to the rhythm. "Have you ever seen the movie *This Is Spinal Tap*?"

"I've heard of it."

"You'd love it. It's a mockumentary making fun of rock bands."

"Who are we going to visit?" I asked then, changing the subject.

"Keli. She's an old friend of mine who lived in my apartment building after college."

Keli, he told me, used to ride around on her mechanized wheelchair with an American flag flying from the handlebar and a handgun stuffed in the chair pocket for self-defense. She struggled with diabetes, obesity, osteoporosis, heart disease, and emphysema and could barely see five feet in front of her. Her family was mostly absent and dysfunctional. After they met, Steve every day started counting her pills for her, making her sandwiches, and keeping her company. He described his friendship with her in a matter-of-fact way and without guile. As we were getting out of the car, I felt a sudden swell of affection for a man who could discuss Christian archeology and Brit pop music in one conversation, a man who took time every Sunday afternoon to visit an old woman in an adult-care facility.

During college, I knew, Steve had volunteered every week with an organization that took care of semi-homeless people living downtown in the slum-run hotels near the railroad tracks. He had a reputation for compassion, and I was attracted to that reputation. More than just reminding me of my history as the child of Quaker missionaries, he represented the best of faith. A man who took care of the disenfranchised was a man worth having. He must know something about God, I thought. He must know something about the mystery of love in a lost world.

Following Steve into a small apartment that smelled of cats and cigarettes, I saw an obese woman sitting at a small round table. She was probably 5'2" and weighed 250 pounds. I could tell she hadn't moved in a long time. Next to her sat an oxygen machine, cigarette butts, and a stack of cheap paperback novels.

"Hi, son," she said, putting out her cigarette. "How are you?"

"Hi, Keli." Steve gave her a hug. "This is Andrea."

She shook my hand. "Steve's a good man, you know

that? When I lived in the city, he used to come down and make me bologna sandwiches. That's what I always want— bologna sandwiches."

She held out her fingers. "See my nails? I love to have my nails painted, but the polish is wearing off. Will you do it for me?"

"I'm not very good at it, but sure."

I took the jar of red polish that she handed me and sat down beside her. Making slow, halting brush strokes, I painted the fingernails of her left hand.

"That's nice, thank you," Keli said. She turned to Steve. "She's a good one, Steve, a keeper." I blushed and bit my lip, embarrassed by her public assessment of me.

Leaning forward then with a look of clarity and inten- tionality, then, she whispered, "He's a good man. And you seem like a good person too."

"If doing your nails is all it takes, then okay."

As I painted the rest of Keli's nails, I watched Steve take care of her apartment. He loaded the garbage and changed the cat litter. He checked the windows and made a handful of sandwiches that he stacked in the fridge. Then he sat down at the table with us and talked with Keli for a while. When we got up to leave, Keli said to him, "You're my family."

"I'll see you next week," Steve said.

Watching him lean over to give her a hug in the coil of breathing tubes, I became one pilgrim admiring another. I saw something almost holy in Steve's kindness toward Keli.

I had once read a story about a man who wrote the poet Gerard Manley Hopkins and asked how he, the man writing, could believe. Hopkins wrote back, "Give alms." According to Flannery O'Connor, he meant that God was to be experienced in the act of love for other human beings and that we weren't to get so tangled up with intellectual quandaries that we failed to look for God in that way. Mundane acts of love were unromantic but important for the soul.

Driving back to the city with Steve and watching the Rocky Mountains off in the distance, I felt a new contentment settling in. After all my years of railing against God for the garbage heap of the human condition, I found not an answer to the problem of suffering but a response. I saw God's goodness manifest in the care of one person for another. Somewhere between the cat litter and the nail polish, I witnessed something sacred.

Chapter 19

MY WELTSCHMERTZ

Me with Steve

"My cat knows how to open doors. Can you believe it?" Keli said to me one Sunday afternoon.

"How?"

"She puts her paw up on the doorknob." Fiddling with her charm bracelet, she said, "Can you help me take this off?" I unlatched it and then dropped it on the table, a coil of cheap silver next to an ashtray.

"Do you miss Steve?" she asked.

"I'm afraid I'll lose him to grad school. He's so hard to read sometimes."

"He likes you," she said, trying to assure me.

"I know he likes me, but does he like me enough?"

"He's a good man." It was like her mantra. "You can trust him."

A few weeks before, I had stood on the sidewalk in front of Steve's apartment building and watched him climb into a U-Haul truck with his Honda mounted behind on a trailer. He was headed to Arizona for a PhD program. He drove down the street, turned around the corner in a wide arc, and then disappeared. I told him I would take over visiting Keli in his stead. Every week, I drove out to her apartment and listened to her tell stories about her amazing cat, her crazy ex-husband, and why Steve had become for her the best thing since bologna sandwiches on white bread.

Not long after Steve left, Keli was admitted to the hospital with an emphysema attack. I went to the hospital emergency room and found her hooked up to IVs. She looked disheveled and alone. I held her hand for a while and talked with her over the din of the ER while doctors came and went, dragging back the curtain on its long chain track.

"Keli's in the hospital," I said to Steve on the phone the next day. I was taking my lunch break at work. "I thought you should know."

We hadn't talked in weeks. When he first left, Steve passed into a no-man's land of distance and transition. Some relationship ambivalence was probably in the mix too. He didn't communicate at all. I was the first one to make contact. Brought together by the tenuous health of a mutual friend, we talked about Keli and then hung up. The call was awkward and brief. But then like an oscillating scale that finally gets tipped in a clear direction, Steve and I started talking on the phone every week. We dated from a distance for four months while he studied and I worked.

After he had settled into his graduate program, Steve flew up to Spokane to see me for a weekend. We spent Saturday afternoon playing Frisbee at a park and talking at a nearby coffee shop. Then we went out for dinner at a restaurant. Over dinner, I told the story of my junior high prom date with Joel Edminster. We had our picture taken at an Old Western photo studio, Joel holding a pistol and wearing a cowboy hat with me sitting on a chair looking stern. After the photo, Joel took me to the gondolas for a ride over the Big Spokane River.

"His mother had to chaperone us on our gondola ride because we were underage," I said. "It was both quaint and mortifying."

Steve laughed.

After dinner, we drove down to the Japanese gardens near the restaurant and found the gate already closed for the night.

"Let's go in anyway," he said, looking at me with a devious expression. I liked him more, just then, for being the kind of person who would break the rules once in a while. Joining his hands in a foothold, he helped vault me over the fence into the garden and then came after. A half-moon was up. After walking past the pagodas, the Japanese maples, and the bamboo thickets, we sat down on a bench.

For the first time, we seemed fully at ease together, sitting in the dark watching the moon's reflection floating on the koi pond.

We kissed that night, not at the gardens — that was too cliché and obvious — but on the cheap ugly futon in my apartment. I felt at peace. Staying up late into the night, we sat together and talked, divulging our pasts and peeling back the onion skins. Steve told me about his parents' painful divorce, his ex-girlfriend, and his tendency to act detached in relationships. I told him about the good and the bad of Ty and Michael, about my broken hearts, the ménage à trois, the getting drunk and losing myself. Some of those choices I wouldn't want repeated by anyone, I said. Other experiences were healthy and normal. Still others in a strange way were both healthy and unhealthy, in the sense that beauty can emerge from dysfunction.

"I made mistakes. Some of them I regret and some I don't," I said.

"When we first got together, I thought you might have a story. I'd rather get the passionate and battle-damaged Andrea than an aloof and lily-white Andrea."

"I'm very human."

"It's who you are. It's what I like about you."

"I know without a doubt that I wouldn't be dating you if I hadn't gone through some of those experiences. This is who I am; this is what I bring with me, all this history."

Steve looked me in the eye. "Your scars make you beautiful."

Just then, I experienced something I hadn't since my baptism, when my youth pastor said my name after he bent me down beneath the river current. In the deepest way, I felt known and understood. I felt a sense of belonging. I felt the blessing of someone taking my search in stride and coming alongside me.

■ ■ ■

"Steve is like an oak tree," Jerry said, sitting in his rocking chair one afternoon when I stopped by to visit. "His roots go very deep. He's grounded, stable."

"More grounded than the men I've picked before, at least."

"*That's* an understatement," Jerry said, knowing some of my dating history.

In the wake of my spiritual crisis, I had started settling into community again. I went to the Sittsers. I stopped by my older brother's house, took my dad to a kitschy Neil Diamond concert with free tickets given out at my work, and cooked dinner with my mom in her kitchen. Steve and I, too, had started easing deeper into community with each other. We talked on the phone more frequently. We wrote in shared journals that we sent to each other in the mail. We flew back and forth every few months for weekend visits.

After Steve took a few trips up to Spokane, I flew down to see him in Arizona one Friday morning. As my plane descended at the Phoenix airport, I saw city spreading out in every direction and, beyond that, desert mountains and miles of saguaro cacti. Steve picked me up from the airport in the same Honda hatchback that he'd been driving for years. While he sat in class that afternoon, I read books in a secluded courtyard near the philosophy building. In the evening, we spent time together in his studio apartment. I got to know the habits of my bachelor boyfriend when he offered to "make" me dinner. After opening the kitchen cupboard, he pointed to a row of canned soup and asked, "Which one?"

On Saturday, we spent most of the day hiking together around the red rock buttes of a nearby park. Late in the day, we drove to the video game arcade at the mall. Steve spent most of his day studying modal logic, so for him, blowing up simulated cars and playing Pac-Man on a vintage game machine was like therapy for his tired brain. After playing at the arcade, making dinner in his windowless kitchen, and then kissing on the couch, we went to a pub near his apartment for a beer. We talked the whole time about faith and philosophy.

Rather than coming to an end, my search had simply been folded into the communal space of our dating relationship. We had all these heady conversations that might to an outsider have seemed contrived, pretentious, or boring. But to us they were the greatest intimacy we shared, two people moving deeper into the private rooms of each other's thoughts and questions. We talked about the meaningful difference between holy and profane and the less-than-meaningful difference between sacred and secular, which by then I finally understood as a false dichotomy. The threshold of the house wasn't either/or; it was both/and. All truth is God's truth, according to the Christian philosopher Arthur Holmes.

We talked, too, about the problem of evil. By then, my

obsession with suffering had become a joke between us. When Steve called on his cell phone from the airport to tell me he'd arrived safely in Spokane for one of his visits, he would say in his dry way that "the jet did not go up in flames *this* time," as I expected, and would I please come and pick him up? I was the committed pessimist between us. He started calling me his "little Weltschmertz," German for "world pain," defined in the dictionary as "a mental depression caused by comparison of the actual state of the world with an ideal state." For me, suffering was still the most profound problem of life and faith.

"When I was a kid," I said, "I used to lie on my back in bed trying really hard to imagine what the universe was like before anything existed, before God existed, trying to imagine *nothingness*. I imagined it as this black, lifeless void."

"You were a philosopher at a young age," Steve said, as we walked past a bar on Mill Street called The Library. After talking at the pub for a while, we had gone out for a walk in downtown Tempe.

"Sometimes I think the problem of evil in a strange, counterintuitive way actually points toward God," I said, "like the human experience is *too* dark to be meaningless."

"What do you mean, exactly?"

"If we lived in a godless world, I would expect to feel physical pain. We'd be all body, no soul. But I wouldn't expect the kind of intense, existential pain that we experience as part of the human condition. *That* kind of suffering seems like it could exist only in a world where God exists, where the soul exists."

Steve nodded.

"The loss we feel must mean something. It's too pointed to be meaningless," I said, remembering AIDS orphans and lonely diabetics. "It's like there's a tearing apart, a sense of incompleteness."

"We've been separated from the ultimate Good."

"Yes."

"Believing that we're just cosmic accidents, that there's nothing spiritual or nonphysical about us, means that suffering has less poignancy and meaning. Is that what you mean?" Steve asked.

"Yes, that's it. There's the nothingness that I imagined as a child lying in bed, and I don't want to live my life that way. It feels soulless."

As I talked for a while, Steve walked beside me and listened. I was taking him into the deepest part of my self—my longing for God. The yearning felt again like a kind of grief. At the very core of my being, I refused to believe that sadness could be explained as a neurochemical response and suffering as just another part of survival in a godless, animal world. Even the darkness in a strange way seemed imbued with something transcendent and sublime.

"I believe in the pain," I said. "I believe in it because I think it *means* something about the soul, about goodness. It makes me long for God and feel angry at God all at the same time."

I stopped talking, then, as we walked down to a long bridge spanning an arc over the dark water of a lake. I thought about my dad and all the conversations we'd had when I was a teenager. I thought about the man I was starting to love who could carry those questions with me, this nerdy bachelor who wore pleated pants and ate canned soup for dinner. I found a companion the way Pilgrim in *The Pilgrim's Progress* finds Hopeful. In Steve, I saw the *imago Dei*, the echo of holiness in the human soul.

In that sense, he seemed like the only means through which I might ever know God. And maybe that was enough too, I thought. Walking together with him that night, I felt God's silence on us not as indifference but as the deepest, most enduring love.

Chapter 20

WHAT CHURCH SHOULD FEEL LIKE

Me editing the Sudan project

At the time that I worked there, the company's main editing suite was a room that had been designed by a film-set artist to look something like the cockpit in a Star Wars spaceship. Faux beams and metal bolts lined the walls. Everything was painted in sleek, silver paint. At the narrow nose of the room sat a huge monitor (the windshield) and below it two computer screens and an editing system (the flight controls).

For a while, that spaceship became my home away from home as I worked after hours on a project for my little brother. Almost every evening at five o'clock, I picked up my mail from home, swung through a Taco Bell for three cheap tacos, and then drove back to work. I sat in the editing suite for hours, culling through footage until one or two in the morning.

One night after I had settled in with my tacos, shoveling cheese into my mouth with one hand and working the computer mouse with the other hand, one of my work colleagues stopped by. Standing in the doorway of the spaceship, he took one glance at the content on my monitor and said, "This doesn't look commercial."

I turned to him with a smile. "It isn't. That's the whole point."

"What is it, then?"

"A documentary about the war in Sudan," I said, letting out a secret that only seemed like a secret, I think because it seemed so personal to me. "My brother's over there."

Before Nathan had boarded a plane for East Africa on his way to do relief work in Sudan, I had said goodbye in the living room of my parents' house. Looking across the room at him and crying, I felt what some people feel when they send their soldier son or brother off to a war zone on another continent. "Dear God, please don't let him die." He was the youngest in the family. My better self. My ruddy-cheeked baby brother going off to a different kind of battle.

Before he left, Nate and I had talked about producing a documentary about the civil war in Sudan. My immediate boss, feeling the same dissonance with the New Orleans conference that I did, had shifted the focus of our division away from cable entertainment and more toward PBS-style programming. I asked his permission to use company equipment to edit the Sudan program in my own time. (We had no budget.) He gave his full support. With a plan in place, I sent Nathan with instructions on how to conduct interviews, how to record good audio, and how to get quality cover footage.

Over the course of his year in Sudan, Nate sent me digital videotapes every few months that would come to me at the company address stuffed in manila envelopes and marked "international mail." After work, I would load each tape into the computer and watch exactly what my little brother had been watching through the camera lens just a few weeks before—a baby getting treatment for malaria at a refugee camp; a UN plane landing on an airstrip to deliver food supplies; a Land Rover driving through arid savanna land. Over weeks and months, I spent almost all my free time organizing Nate's footage into a documentary.

When Nathan came back from East Africa a year later, I was still busy working on the project. My parents, my older brother, and I drove over to the Seattle-Tacoma International Airport together and stood waiting in the terminal. We saw him ascending up the long escalator, looking haggard. He'd lost a lot of weight. As my mom hugged him, she cried the way I imagine any mother might cry if her youngest kid had gone off to war and managed to avoid being blown up by land mines.

Although I didn't cry, I teared up when I saw him. I felt a swell of pride for my little brother. I also felt a little bit of envy. I wanted what I thought he had—a unified sense of faith and life purpose. Nothing was ever that simple, of course. I knew better. Back in Spokane, Nathan told me over coffee about his time in Sudan and all the questions that had surfaced about faith, prayer, and humanitarian work.

"It's a hard thing for me to work through," he said. "When people ask me what they can do to help, I tell them to send money or volunteer, and I tell them to pray. But both are difficult."

"What do you mean?"

He paused, tapped his paper cup on the table, and then looked up at me.

"I believe in praying and in doing good, but sometimes I'm not sure they make a whit of difference."

"They seem pointless sometimes, don't they?"

"The problems of the world mount before us and what can we do?"

"We keep trying," I said.

"We keep praying," he said.

I felt the same dilemma Nate did. When I first took on the Sudan video project, I had volunteered partly out of love for him and partly out of love for Africa, my first home. But I also needed a way to reintegrate my past and present—the missionary kid with the movie producer. Maybe I was trying to fulfill my mother's Great Commission to "go M.A.D." (make a difference). Maybe I was doing penance for silly advertisements I'd helped to produce. Or maybe after so much criticism about what was wrong with the church and the world, I felt some compensatory need to quit complaining and start *doing* something. The search wasn't just about finding love and faith, it was also about looking for life purpose. Why am I here? Does what I do on a daily basis *mean* anything?

By then, I had culled through probably fifty hours of Nate's footage, eaten scores of tacos, and taken three trips. After a couple of private donors came through for the project, I'd flown to Los Angeles to interview the British director of a nonprofit operating in Sudan and then to Washington, D.C., to interview the director of The Center for Religious Freedom, as well as a Sudanese research professor of international politics, law, and society at The Johns Hopkins University. I'd also driven over to Seattle with a small crew to interview half a dozen refugees who had been granted asylum by the US government.

The very last interview I did was with Nathan. He was the first and the last—the first person who had started the project with me and the last story I heard. He looked less haggard by the time of the interview. In the company studio, I sat next to the cameraman and Nate sat opposite me with a small lavaliere microphone pinned to his shirt. For an hour, he talked about the politics of aid work and about the volunteer work he'd done with refugees and what it meant to him. He looked both vulnerable and confident sitting there under the stare of the studio lights, disclosing his heart.

"It changes the way I see the world," he said, looking me straight in the eye with the look of fierce clarity that reminded me of why I loved him so much. "I see the world differently because of the way that *they* have seen the world.

I've heard their voices and I carry their voices with me every day." I wanted to get up right then and hug Nathan, tell him that I was so glad to be his sister. He gave me hope.

After his interview, I loaded the tapes into my system and stayed up for almost six hours after an already long workday. My eyes burned from staring at the monitor for so long. Next to me on the console sat books on the history of the civil war in Sudan, a scratch pad with time code marks, and stacks of tapes. I was the only person in the building except for a night-shift editor, who around midnight tip-toed up to the doorway of my room trying to scare me in the dark.

"Andromeda Precipice," he whispered in his deep bari-tone voice, sustaining the last *c* in *precipice* like Gollum in The Lord of the Rings. "Andromeda Precipice" was a strange nickname he'd derived from the first letters of my first and last name.

"Don't do that," I said, catching my breath as he walked down the hall to his own editing room. Both of us were like miners working alone in our underground caves.

After finishing Nate's studio tapes, I started transcribing parts of an interview that he'd conducted with a Sudanese hospital chaplain who lost her daughter and husband to the war. She didn't know if they were dead or alive or out lost in the desert trying to survive against invading militias. For the interview, the chaplain sat in a chair up against a mud hut wall. Afternoon light cut shafts behind her. Although I couldn't see him, I pictured Nate sitting across from her behind his tripod. I could hear his voice off camera asking questions of someone he seemed to know and care about.

"Do you think about them all the time?" he asked quietly, referring to her husband and daughter. Before the chaplain answered, a small aircraft went flying overhead. The chaplain stopped and listened. Nathan paused.

"I have to listen carefully, if it's an Antonov," she said, referring to the military aircraft purchased on the Russian black market and used for bombing raids on civilians.

"How do you know the sound of an Antonov?" Nathan asked.

"It comes heavy, and isn't low. It's high," she said, raising her hand in the air.

"How many times have you been present during a bombing?"

She paused. "No, I have forgotten how many."

In one part of their conversation about Antonovs, the audio was distorted and hard to hear. I called up Nate and had him come over to my apartment the next day so that we could recreate an acoustic environment similar to the one in which the original clip had been recorded. My bathroom, of all things, did the trick. I stood next to the sink recording on a small miniDV camera while Nathan stood in the shower.

"How many times have you been present during a bombing?" he said.

"Again," I said.

"How many times have you been present during a bombing?"

"One more time."

"How many times have you been present during a bombing?"

"Perfect, that's all I need," I said.

For a few minutes, I had to focus on the technicalities of getting good audio. But then, as I shut the camera off, I found myself having a moment of sober realization. A second ago, I had just been standing with my leg propped casually on a toilet seat while my brother leaned against a bathtub wall repeating a line about terrorist atrocities on another continent. The whole exchange seemed surreal and unnerving.

Back at work with my new audio clip, I listened to the chaplain tell her story again in more detail. I thought, My God, this woman lost her only child during the chaos of a raid, literally lost her on the plains of south Sudan. It was horrifying. And yet the chaplain didn't have the kind of hollow countenance I expected of someone who listened for the sound pitch of a Russian Antonov right after being reminded of her missing kid. She talked about serving others as a chaplain. As she spoke, her face had a look of calm that seemed almost holy.

I wasn't so Christian. All of a sudden I felt like yelling obscenities and cursing God for all the grief that people go through in their lives. I felt like giving up. Why try? Why believe in God's goodness, if so much seemed withheld? After fighting the same despair in the slums of Nairobi, I'd sorted things out for a while. I'd had an epiphany, or two or three. I'd gained some clarity. But now the old demons were back again.

For that night and all the nights that came after, I sat in my Star Wars cockpit, confused and alone, out hovering in the darkness between warring planets and death stars.

■ ■ ■

When the documentary was finished, I sent copies to the director of the nonprofit organization that had hosted my brother for his year in Sudan. I gave a copy to my parents and to Nathan and sent a copy to Damon, who was back in the Bay Area working at a movie theater and trying to write. I sent a copy to the organizer of the Amnesty International Film Festival in Victoria, B.C., who heard about the film and wanted me to show it at their upcoming festival.

I also gave a copy to the audio-visual director at Knox for an event that Nathan and I had been planning for months — a premiere that would take place not at a theater but at a church. I don't remember who suggested that we show the film in the sanctuary. For reasons that didn't fully illuminate themselves until the event, it turned out to be the right place to show the documentary.

My mother, our informal agent and publicist, told all her friends about the showing. My father told his colleagues at work. Nate and I put announcements in the church bulletin and sent out emails to faculty and students at Whitworth. We told friends to come and told them to tell *their* friends to come.

On the night of the event, somewhere around 150 or 200 people showed up at the church, filling the pews in a way that they hadn't been filled in years. At seven o'clock, I gave a brief introduction, cued the audio-visual director, and then found my seat. Hearing the projector hum from the balcony and watching the beam of light sift across the space of the sanctuary, I was reminded of watching *The Pilgrim's Progress* on the old reel-to-reel projector in the Lugulu hospital ward. Twenty years had gone by since then. I was on my own pilgrimage, now, sitting in a church pew again and watching a film I'd sunk myself into for the last year.

After the film finished, Nathan and I walked up onto the sanctuary stage along with two Whitworth faculty that we had invited to join us in a post-viewing discussion panel. One was a professor of politics who specialized in peace studies and international politics, and the other, a professor of psychology who specialized in the study of genocide and human evil. The panel members introduced themselves and gave a brief commentary on the film. Then we opened up a question-and-answer forum.

About halfway down the sanctuary, a man from Knox stood up and asked, "The discovery of oil has coincided with the increased oppression of the south, has it not?" He worked for a time as a midlevel manager in a major oil company and understood the complexities of oil, money, and politics. Across the aisle from him, a family friend of mine stood up. She was a retired English professor. She also directed a Christian nonprofit that equipped young people to serve in the inner city and around the world in support of social justice and environmental causes. "In what ways has the UN been involved in peacekeeping in Sudan?" she wanted to know.

Then sitting way at the back of the sanctuary under the balcony where Spiderman had once leapt off during the summer VBS skit, another woman raised her hand and stood up. She was a former journalist turned stay-at-home mom who attended Knox with her family. "So much suffering goes on in the world," she said. "I'm just a mother of four children living in a city nowhere near Sudan. I care, but I feel overwhelmed by caring and powerless to make a difference. What can I do?"

I don't remember who on the panel gave an answer to that question or any of the others. To me, what mattered more than the quality of response was the quality of inquiry. People in the church were asking smart, incisive questions, even if there were no easy answers. The whole discussion carried with it a sense that all of us were seeing "through a glass darkly," as Paul says in 1 Corinthians. I thought of my neighbor Will taping magazine pictures on his cupboard. "I want to remember," he said, "how other people live. What my choices mean."

Looking out at the audience that evening, I took note of all the people who had come—Jerry, along with other former professors; Steve, up visiting from Arizona; my parents, my older brother and his family; my boss from work, who'd supported the project. Lots of Knox church members had come, as well, among them Scott Edminster; Jason, the former youth pastor who co-taught junior high Sunday school with me; and Cathy, my friend who worked at the cemetery. The Knox community was present the way it had always been present, supporting and celebrating my life at birthday parties, baptisms, and film screenings.

In the audience, too, I saw people who didn't attend church at all, people outside the tradition of faith. They were friends of my parents and other friends of friends who had been invited. One of them was a colleague of my dad's, a seeking agnostic who had no interest in institutional religion but would stop by my dad's office at work and ask serious, probing questions about faith and metaphysics.

Looking around the sanctuary that night, I thought, This is what church should feel like—people of all kinds coming together to ask questions about what it means to be human. I felt a sense of homecoming. I wasn't standing anxiously on the threshold looking out or looking in. I was moving deeper inside the house. The house had its faults; God knows I had spent time criticizing those faults. And yet for me I also associated the church with the pursuit of truth and justice, with community and shared humanity. It was a place to ask the unanswerable questions and a place to be on sojourn. Maybe, in that sense, the search was no longer something outside the church but rather a vast, open country within.

Into that country I carried the stones of my heart and laid them on the sanctuary altar. I hadn't stopped asking questions. Not at all. I brought them as my only offering to God, as if to say, This film, about death and war and suffering, belongs here in the church. All my other questions, too, belong here. I want to ask them in this place. I want to ask them in this community. And God, I don't know what I think of you. I don't know what I think of Christ. I don't know what I think of this stink of the human condition. But I'll come, anyway. Along with my longing, I'll bring my doubts and my questions. I'll wait for you here. I'll call this place home.

Chapter 21

ALL I NEED
IS A LAND ROVER

Me with Ruth, far right

Six months or so after I had started going back to church,
my mother and I walked out of Knox one Sunday morning
and ran into an old woman trying to sell hand-crocheted
baby booties. She begged in broken English for us to buy
them. I could tell from her accent that she was Russian.
Spokane has a large Russian immigrant population. After
digging through her purse to pick from the assortment of
booties, I bought a pair and then walked out to the parking

lot with my mother. After we had driven about three blocks from the church, I turned to her from the passenger seat and said, "Go back. We have to go back." She thought something was wrong.

"What's the matter?"

"We have to buy more booties."

"Are you serious?"

"We have to go back," I said again. The woman was trying to make a living. She was working for it. She was poor.

My mother turned the car around, but after pulling into the church parking lot again, we couldn't find the woman anywhere. For almost twenty minutes, I made my mom drive through the neighborhood as I looked down every alleyway and street for the diminutive figure of an old Russian woman carrying a bag of booties. We never found her. But the next Sunday when she showed up outside the church with her beat-up leather purse, I bought another pair of booties. The Sunday after that, too, I bought a pair. I was acting on a surge of pity the way a ten-year-old might, except that I was twenty-five years old.

While growing up in Kenya, I had somehow developed the misguided belief, what some might call the "missionary complex," that the world required saving and I was the one who would save it. All I needed was a big heart and a spare tire for my Land Rover. The Land Rover was the iconic car of the rural missionary and the car of choice when I grew up and became serious about changing the world. "Changing the world" seemed like an actual vocation that I could select someday when graduating from college, a job that my career counselor would recommend after assessing my career questionnaire, the profession I could someday print on my business cards.

Years later, as a young adult, that missionary complex still plagued me. My conscience was the size of a prize-winning watermelon. Before brushing my teeth at night, I would notice the toothpaste was out. Throwing it away reminded me of a garbage dump and a garbage dump made me think of starving children. When a telemarketer called asking for my business, I felt sorry for her too, as she tried to make a living. I carried Taco Bell gift certificates in my purse to hand to homeless people the way my mother used to carry loaves of bread in her bag when she went to market in Lugulu. The world needed saving, one beggar at a time, one bootie at a time.

And yet, for all my missionary kid dreams of saving the world from war and famine, I was living an unremarkable life trying to find love and community not for others but for myself, mostly. I was a Mother Teresa wannabe, a fan without follow-through. During the Q&A portion of the Sudan showing, I had talked about a novel in which the main character gets so caught up in foreign philanthropy that she neglects her own kids. Even though it might seem less sensational than going overseas to someone else's war— although that was important too—we had to take care of our own communities. "We need to be present to the pain in our own back yards," I said to the audience, thinking, Okay, but how do I do this myself?

After the Sudan project was over and I had more time on my hands, I did research trying to find an organization to volunteer with. One Sunday while perusing the bulletin during a sermon, I noticed an announcement for an interdenominational consortium of Christian churches dedicated to housing the homeless. The organization was called Interfaith Hospitality Network of Spokane. Once a month, they needed two people from the hosting church to stay overnight with the homeless families. This is perfect, I thought, stuffing the bulletin into my purse.

On the first night that I volunteered, I packed a small bag and drove down the hill to Knox. The parking lot was empty except for one other car and a large van. Inside in the fellowship hall, two homeless families were using the space as if it were the living room of a house. Next to the small pulpit on the far side of the hall, a little boy slouched on a chair watching the dull hum and flicker of a television. At one of the tables, a father sat feeding peas to his toddler. In the kitchen adjoining the hall, where the church matriarchs used to make tea and coffee for the congregation, two women were milling around cooking, as if it were just a regular kitchen.

I stood in the doorway of the fellowship hall, watching everything for a moment. Then I walked in, set down my backpack, and introduced myself. One of the kids, a girl who looked about twelve, introduced herself as Ruth.

"That's a very biblical name," I said.

Ruth started telling me all about her family, where she was from, and why her cousin Heaven was in town. "Heaven is only staying with us because there's no room in Idaho," she said, referring to family who lived across the state line. "They've been kicked out of their apartment but are hoping to find another apartment soon."

After Ruth ran off to play with her brother, I walked into the kitchen. Ruth's mom and another mother were making sloppy joes for the two families. While leaning up against the kitchen counter watching her stir ground beef in a frying pan, I listened to her talk about the family and the tumult going on. They had a legal hearing to attend the next day.

"Ruth's stepdad's on trial for raping her. We have to go to court," she said, matter-of-factly, as if going to court were the thing you did after picking up your kids from school and before taking them to baseball practice. I listened for a while without talking. Then I walked out of the kitchen to find Ruth, who suddenly seemed older and more wounded to me than thirty minutes before when I had first met her.

"Do you want to see the bomb shelter?" I asked, trying to think of something imaginative for the child who'd been robbed of her childhood.

"Yes!" she said, clapping her hands together.

With Ruth following behind, I turned the corner into the long corridor behind the fellowship hall. For years, the church janitor had used it as an informal storage closet for mops and tools and cleaning supplies. At the very end of the corridor, hanging on a rolling track, was an eight-foot-high sliding door made of heavy wood and covered in mismatched sheet metal.

"This is it," I said to Ruth. Grabbing ahold of the handle, I leaned back to leverage my weight and then pulled open the door. Just inside was a light switch that I flicked on to illuminate the cement staircase leading down into the room. I hadn't seen it in years. Built in 1888, Knox during the '20s had added a boiler room in the basement that was used to store rations during the Cold War. Even though the gym had been designated as the formal bomb shelter, as kids, we called the boiler room the bomb shelter. The whole room smelled of something old and dank. It looked like a dungeon. Shelves lined the old stone-and-mortar walls. Half burned-out fluorescent bulbs hung from the high ceiling and left a green, eerie glow in the windowless room.

I remembered standing at the top of those stairs as a kid, feeling chilled with the intrigue of war, apocalypse, and eating canned food for days on end. Over time, the Knox kids had developed an unspoken understanding that if all hell broke loose in the world, we would come to church carrying our backpacks and clutching our lunch pails. Together, we would descend down into the heart of the bomb shelter. We would sleep in sleeping bags, play with flashlights in the dark, and eat canned peaches off the shelves for weeks. We would drink Kool-Aid, too, which we had remembered at the last minute to grab from the kitchen. Knox was our home base in case of dire emergency. That was how I thought of church back then—as my safe place, my refuge.

"We used to play down here when I was a kid," I said to Ruth. "We played hide-and-seek and another game called aliens. Do you want to play one of those games?"

"Hide-and-seek," she said.

After tracking down her brother and a few other kids, we ran around the four floors of the church in the same way the Knox kids and I used to roam that space. After a while, Ruth's mother called us to dinner in the fellowship hall. The other volunteer said a prayer. One of the homeless mothers started passing plates of food around. One of the fathers passed the salt and pepper. For an hour, we sat at the table together eating sloppy joes and talking.

After the dishes had been washed and dried and put away, we all went to bed in our separate corners of the building. Cheap cots had been rolled into each room and linens left folded on each cot. I had been assigned to the choir room, a wide-open space that seemed nothing like a bedroom except for the cot sitting in the middle of it. On the other side of the wall was the old pastor's office where I had once sat for my prebaptismal preparation. Across the hallway was the sanctuary where I had started attending service again every Sunday.

All night long I tossed and turned on my cot, waking now and then to think about the homeless baby sleeping in a crib in the Sunday school room down the hall or the girl with the cousin named Heaven. Wedged between a closet of Presbyterian choir robes and an old church piano, I felt strangely at home.

PART EIGHT

THE DELECTABLE MOUNTAINS

From the House Beautiful, Pilgrim can
see forward to the Delectable Mountains
and other terrain that he will cross through
on his journey. Standing at the House
Beautiful, Pilgrim has yet a long road in
front of him.

Chapter 22

A PASSING LIGHT

A year and a half after Steve and I started dating, Keli was taken to the hospital again. I was visiting her one Sunday afternoon when she started into a fit of violent coughing. I saw panic in her eyes and called 911. Ten minutes later, three men came through the front door carrying their nylon bags. They rolled her onto a gurney and then hauled her out the door to the hospital.

When she was released, Keli called and asked me to come and take her home. I drove to the hospital and, along with a nurse, pushed her wheelchair out the doors of the Emergency Room and then hoisted her heavy frame into the passenger seat of my car. As I drove east toward the Valley, Keli asked me to pull over and stop at a convenience mart.

"I need cigarettes," she said.

"Keli, you just got out of the hospital from an emphysema attack. Cigarettes are killing you."

"It's too late. I need cigarettes."

I remembered something Steve had told me, how futile it was to have this conversation with her over and over. She was an old woman addicted to nicotine. In these dying days, I thought, let her have her Virginia Slims. I pulled into the convenience mart, took the cash she handed me, and then bought a pack of cigarettes from the clerk behind the counter.

Two weeks later Keli was back in the hospital, admitted this time to the Providence Sacred Heart Medical Center right next to my apartment building. My dad had worked at that same Catholic hospital for the last twenty years after coming back from Kenya.

After Keli was admitted, I stopped by every day to visit her on my way home. The visits became a source of comfort to me. I needed company as much as she did. After work in the evening, I would drop coins in a streetside parking meter, ride the elevator to the fifth floor, and go down the hall to see an old and passing friend. Keli's room looked out over the city the way my apartment did, except her view faced directly east toward the mountains instead of north. In front of her window was a wide ledge where the nurses put cards and flowers, the few that came.

The first night that I stopped by to visit, I brought Keli a small Bonsai plant that I set in the window ledge next to the cards and the wilted cut flowers.

"I had a dream last night," Keli said as I stood by her bedside. "There were cherry tomatoes falling out of my IV."

"That's funny."

"I like the plant you brought. It looks like a tiny tree."

"It's called a Bonsai. I thought you might want something other than flowers."

I brought it over for her to look at, then set it back in the window when the nurse came in with a dinner plate. Keli asked me to help feed her dinner; her hands were trembling too much. I fed her baked chicken and mashed potatoes and, for dessert, fruit in cottage cheese, one spoonful at a time. Halfway through dessert, I found myself crying into her cottage cheese. Watching her die felt both painful and mundane. She couldn't go to the bathroom. She couldn't walk. She had to be spoon-fed the way a baby has to be spoon-fed.

"Take care of the Bonsai for me when I'm gone; don't let it die," she said.

"You're still here, Keli."

"Yes, but not for long."

For almost an hour, we sat together by her bed that night. I held her clawlike hand. She cracked jokes about her catheter and sassed the nurses. As we talked, we half-watched reruns of *Murder, She Wrote* on the hospital TV that was mounted on the wall above her bed. Watching that show became one of the rituals of my visits, the way it became a ritual for me to water the plants on her windowsill and throw away the wilted flowers once a week. Sometimes my dad came by if he knew I was at the hospital. With his doctor's coat flapping behind him, he would stop into the room, take Keli by the hand, and ask her how she was feeling today.

One night after visiting Keli in the hospital, I went home and called her from my apartment. I told her I thought she might be able to see *my* window from *her* window.

"Look south toward the cathedral," I said. "Do you see that?" I flicked my living room lights on and off like Morse code from a ship at sea.

289

"I can see you! I can see you!" she said, flicking her room light on and off. She laughed like a child and I laughed with her.

The next day, I went to visit Keli again but found an empty room. A nurse told me she'd been moved to another facility called St. Luke's. After driving to St. Luke's, I walked down the long corridors of the nursing home until I found Keli's room. I sat at her bedside talking with her for a while until the nurses came in to help her take a bowel movement. The process involved three people lifting her body off the bed and into a sling toilet. Watching it was more than I could handle. I felt overwhelmed by her need and recoiled the way I'd recoiled from the orphan who peed and smeared pus all over me in the Nairobi orphanage.

"I'm going to go home, Keli," I said.

She held out her arms from behind the bustle of nurses, begging me to stay, pleading after me as I turned and walked out of the room.

"I need to go home," I said again.

That moment was the last time I saw her conscious. The next day, Keli's mind went underground, and the day after that she died. As I walked into her room, I stopped cold at the empty bed. A nurse behind me said in a sad, pragmatic voice, "Keli died this morning." My heart stung. Taking the Bonsai tree from her windowsill, I went home feeling lost by her death and by the fact that I'd abandoned her in the last hours. My courage had failed. At the time when it really mattered, I didn't know how to be a Christian. I left her hanging in a toilet sling.

While sitting on my futon that night, I called Steve in Arizona and in between long, grief-stricken pauses, told him that Keli had died. Two days later, I drove to the funeral home for the prefuneral viewing and was ushered into a room where Keli's body lay on a table. I had never been alone with a dead body before. The stillness seemed absolute and the distance between us almost tangible, as if I were standing on one side of a chasm with Keli on the other side. She was right there, and yet I couldn't reach her. She was gone.

In Steve's place, my dad came with me to the funeral that weekend at a small country graveyard off the I-90 freeway. When it came time for people to share their parting words, I didn't have the heart to say anything. My dad said a word on our behalf while I cried into my gray wool gloves. Standing in the cold winter snow watching her ashes being set down into a small hole in the ground, I thought about Keli experiencing death as a kind of fruition, returning home and being ushered into the great mystery of God.

I believed in the afterlife for Keli and I believed in it for myself. My belief had nothing to do with delusional fantasy or fear of death. It had everything to do with the instincts of my heart. The human condition seemed like a passageway to somewhere else. A throughway to the far-off mountains. What lay on the other side, I didn't know. That experience could only be left to inadequate metaphor. The homing bird after a thousand miles came to the place she'd been looking for, tucked in her outstretched wings, and drifted down out of the wind. Pilgrim walked through the Valley of the Shadow of Death, as David calls it in the Psalms, and then climbed up and over the mountain pass, going home to his final refuge.

On this side of the mountains, God was mostly hidden. But sometimes from a distance light passed between the peaks before things went into shadow again. For me, that light had manifested itself indirectly through art and nature — in hearing a song or seeing a flock of birds ascending in the sky. At other times, the light revealed itself more directly.

Not long before Keli died, I came home one evening from seeing her at the hospital. It was early December. Ice crystals rimmed the windows of my apartment. The floorboard heaters rattled. After dropping my keys on the counter, I sat down at my dining room table to eat dinner and rummage through a pile of bills, junk mail, and Christmas letters. I organized the mail and washed dishes and then by ten o'clock climbed into bed. My sleep was fitful. I tossed and turned, listening to the creak of footsteps overhead. The hum of old water pipes in the walls. The siren of an ambulance passing on the street below. After a while, I fell asleep.

Around midnight, I woke up feeling a slight pressure on my head that I can describe only as that of a hand. I remember lying there in the dark in that muddy stage of early consciousness thinking, Surely this is just a physiological phenomenon. I must have a mild headache. Maybe I'm imagining things. But somewhere in the clearest part of my mind I knew I was feeling the hand of God upon me, like a priest's hand resting on my head while I knelt at the altar. It came as a blessing, just there, just for a moment.

Frederick Buechner, in writing about his own conversion, said, "Something in me recoils to use such language."

I admit too that I recoil in trying to describe this experience. It feels too personal. Too abstract. I grew up around doctors and scientists. I used to associate these kinds of stories with crazy spiritualists or with hippies who had drug-induced run-ins with the numinous. Sharing about it seems at worst like an admission of mental instability and at best like a submission to something out beyond the realm of empirical knowledge. The encounter can't be tested or replicated. And yet, it felt as real to me as if my own father had laid his hand on my head. "The peace that passes understanding" came over me.

I wouldn't describe the experience as a conversion or an epiphany or anything else of that kind. My doubt didn't vanish suddenly and the search didn't resolve. But I did experience that moment of peace. In the solitude of night, I felt a hand gently touching my head, and then after a minute or two I fell asleep again. In that brief waking, my longing abated. My loneliness pushed back like a curtain. Behind the curtain was a window and through the window, a passing light.

Chapter 23

A MELANCHOLY CHRISTIAN

The foothills of the Rocky Mountains

One year after Keli died, Steve flew into town on his Christmas break. He proposed to me on a sunlit hike along the Little Spokane River, not far from where I'd been baptized as a child. The river was laced with ice and brilliant in the winter sun. I said yes for reasons both significant and insignificant: for taking care of an old woman and naming Foreigner on FM radio. For studying philosophy and asking deep questions about life and faith. For being a soul mate and a man I loved. A few months later on a Sunday afternoon at Knox Presbyterian, we stood at the front of the sanctuary together watching Jerry raise his hand to pronounce us husband and wife.

After our honeymoon, Steve and I flew back to Spokane to pack up my apartment before moving to Arizona so that he could finish graduate school. On the night before we left, we sat on my futon for the last time. Across the room in a windowsill, Keli's Bonsai tree sat in its porcelain pot. I had tried to keep it alive. But over time it died slowly, dropping down into a small frail skeleton.

"What would you do if I lost my faith?" I said to Steve, testing him the way I had tested him when I told him that I'd left the church for a while.

"You won't lose your faith," he said.

"How can you be so sure?"

"Because you can't live without hope. It's how you're wired."

"My theistic beliefs are unwavering. I can't get away from my belief in God; I think I know that now. But my Christian beliefs are always wavering."

"That will be your struggle from here on out. Your questions are important because they help people think critically and honestly about their views. They help people pay attention. That's your contribution."

"Maybe so."

"I've gone through times too when I wondered at a really deep existential level, What is this all for? Why did God allow any of this in the first place?"

I nodded. "Life seems so opaque and hard to understand sometimes."

"In one of my periods of doubt, I remember cracking open the Bible and thinking, How could anyone find these theological claims credible?"

"At some point or another, a lot of Christians have probably felt that way," I said.

Jerry had said to me once while standing in the kitchen doing dishes, "God is only looking for a seed of faith, a small, simple thing." I still had so many questions—about the doctrine of atonement, the triune God, the purpose of prayer. Behind those questions were buried other questions. What happens if I lose my faith? If I keep my faith, what will it *look* like? What will it mean?

Before Steve and I were engaged, I had a strange dream in which I was getting married. At the reception, the pastor made his way around the room and, when he got to me, gave me the guest book to sign. He asked me what he had been asking all the wedding guests: "What is your religious affiliation?" With almost involuntary impulse, I wrote down "Christian." But then, dissatisfied with my answer, I called the pastor back. Taking the pen from his hand, I added a qualifier so that my entry read, "Melancholy Christian."

The dream didn't require much in the way of interpretation. I woke up the next morning and while lying in bed thought, I guess that's how I feel about faith. I feel like a melancholy Christian. Nothing fully satisfied my spiritual need—not music, art, or even love. I was waiting for something not yet fully revealed. In the meantime, disbelief took up intermittent rent in the empty space of my heart. And yet that same disbelief made room for belief. My doubt and disappointment came from my longing. My longing came from the *imago Dei*, the mark of God in me.

In one of his poems in *The Book of Pilgrimage*, Rainer Maria Rilke writes,

> Whom should I turn to,
> If not the one whose darkness
> Is darker than the night, the only one
> Who keeps vigil with no candle,
> And is not afraid—
> The deep one, whose being I trust.

The search itself, even with all its dead-end roads, meant something. I was sure of that. And it meant something only if, at the end of all things, I could find the being "whose darkness [was] darker than the night." Faith directed me not away from but *into* my doubt, into those deep spaces of God's dwelling.

■ ■ ■

The morning after we finished packing up my apartment, Steve volunteered to drive the U-Haul. We drove past St. John's Cathedral and the Sacred Heart Medical Center and up onto the I-90 freeway going west. The truck behind us was packed full with furniture, boxes of books, and wooden garden pots with the soil still in them. I had insisted on keeping the soil.

"You have to put your foot down at some point," my

dad said to Steve, jokingly, while we were loading the truck. No one could reason with me. I was attached to my stuff. I wanted to bring it all with me, worthless belongings that weighed a lot and cost money to haul halfway across the country: a small rusted bank vault that I had turned into a plant stand (twenty pounds); bricks that I used to build my bookshelves (a hundred and fifty pounds); canned food that I didn't want to waste (ten pounds). I might as well have been packing for the apocalypse.

Although I was moving only four states away, I felt as if I were moving to another country, the way I had as a seven-year-old kid leaving Kenya. I still remember the exact Burger King we stopped at when we first arrived in Spokane back in 1985. It's stuck in my memory as a symbol of transition, the last stop on a long trip west across America. "This is where we're going to live," my mother had said, rolling down the window of the car to order lunch. Spokane was the end of the road, at least then.

Twenty years later, I climbed into a moving truck with my belongings and started driving west out of the city. It was June. The foothills of the Rocky Mountains were young and green. With the morning sun behind us, we had more than a thousand miles of road ahead of us. Not long after Steve and I started onto I-90, my parents called on my cell phone. "What is it?" I asked. My dad paused. I could tell something was wrong.

"Timone just died," he said. Timone was the son of Moses and Christine Kivunike, our Ugandan friends who fled Idi Amin in the middle of the night. Our families had kept in close touch over the years. I remembered Timone from my childhood as a playmate roaming the Lugulu compound with my brothers and me. For his whole life, he had suffered from sickle-cell disease, and in that sense, his death wasn't unexpected. I didn't feel shock. But I felt grief. Halfway around the world a friend had died, and somehow, that made leaving home that much lonelier.

After I hung up the phone, Steve reached over to hold my hand briefly and then went back to steering the truck. We didn't talk much. I felt his comfort and companionship in the shared silence. Every time the engine changed gears, the weight behind us shifted—the sixteen-foot truck and, behind the truck on a trailer, my light blue Nissan.

"Did you buy a map of Arizona?" I said after a while, turning to Steve.

"It's in the glove compartment."

The road leading west out of Spokane climbed up from the valley and into the high plains of Eastern Washington. Pine trees covered the countryside. After thirty miles or so, the trees began to disappear. The mountains, too, began to vanish in the rear view mirror. Looking forward, the countryside opened up into the dry flatlands of Central Washington. There was nothing but horizon to look at. The desert seemed almost interminable.

"Okay," I said after a long pause. "Here we go."

Credits

For more information about the author and public readings of this book, or to schedule a reading in your city, please visit **andreapalpantdilley.com**.

Share Your Thoughts

With the Author: Your comments will be forwarded to the author when you send them to *zauthor@zondervan.com*.

With Zondervan: Submit your review of this book by writing to *zreview@zondervan.com*.

Free Online Resources at
www.zondervan.com

Zondervan AuthorTracker: Be notified whenever your favorite authors publish new books, go on tour, or post an update about what's happening in their lives at www.zondervan.com/authortracker.

Daily Bible Verses and Devotions: Enrich your life with daily Bible verses or devotions that help you start every morning focused on God. Visit www.zondervan.com/newsletters.

Free Email Publications: Sign up for newsletters on Christian living, academic resources, church ministry, fiction, children's resources, and more. Visit www.zondervan.com/newsletters.

Zondervan Bible Search: Find and compare Bible passages in a variety of translations at www.zondervanbiblesearch.com.

Other Benefits: Register to receive online benefits like coupons and special offers, or to participate in research.

ZONDERVAN®

ZONDERVAN.com/
AUTHORTRACKER
follow your favorite authors